PRAISE FOR "RETHINKING STUDENT TRANSITIONS"

"This book is a much needed and long overdue reframing of transitions that will serve student success and support institutional effectiveness and impact. Steeped in research but still highly accessible to all practitioners, educators, advocates, and scholars, the "transition as becoming" model that Drs. Young and Bunting provide is highly inclusive of "new traditional" student populations, widely applicable to all academic and personal transitions, and poised to truly transform the way we conceptualize, discuss, and study student transitions."

\- **Jennifer R. Keup**, *Vice President of Urban Initiatives, APLU; Executive Director, Coalition of Urban Serving Universities; and Senior Fellow, National Resource Center for The First-Year Experience and Students in Transition*

"Yes! At the exact moment higher ed is grappling with effectively meeting the needs of our multi-faceted students, Young and Bunting shepherd us into the next theoretical era with their finely tuned perspectives. Soon to be a staple in graduate programs and professional development circles, be prepared to think deeply and be rewarded with practical guidance."

\- **Janet L. Marling**, *Executive Director, National Institute for the Study of Transfer Students and Associate Professor of Education, University of North Georgia*

"As administrators, faculty, and staff help college students navigate important experiences and decisions, now is the time for new resources on student transition theory. This book meets that need by pairing relevant and practical concepts with a community-focused approach to prepare professionals for myriad future discussions of students' transitions."

\- **Amelia Parnell**, *President, NASPA – Student Affairs Administrators in Higher Education*

"It is far past time to reimagine the theory and practice of college student transition. Young and Bunting have done just that, advancing a perspective rooted in meaningful community participation that is sure to be generative for researchers and administrators alike."

\- **Rachel A. Smith**, *Assistant Professor of Higher Education and Student Affairs, Iowa State University*

RETHINKING STUDENT TRANSITIONS

How Community, Participation, and Becoming
Can Help Higher Education Deliver on its Promise

DALLIN GEORGE YOUNG

BRYCE D. BUNTING

About the Publisher

The National Resource Center for The First-Year Experience and Students in Transition was born out of the success of University of South Carolina's first-year seminar ("University 101") and a series of annual conferences focused on the first-year experience. The momentum created by the educators and advocates attending these early conferences paved the way for the development of the National Resource Center, which was established at the University of South Carolina in 1986. As the Center broadened its focus to include other significant student transitions in higher education, it underwent several name changes, adopting the National Resource Center for The First-Year Experience and Students in Transition in 1998.

Today, the National Resource Center collaborates with institutional partners in student success, student affairs, and academic units as well as with institutions, organizations, and affiliates across the country and around the world in pursuit of its mission to advance and support efforts to improve student learning and transitions into and through higher education. The Center achieves this mission by creating opportunities for the exchange of practical and scholarly information, facilitating the discussion of trends and issues in our field, and providing thought leadership. Its primary areas of activity include:

- convening conferences and other professional development events such as webinars, workshops, and online learning opportunities

- publishing scholarly practice books, research reports, guides, a peer-reviewed journal, and an electronic newsletter

- generating, supporting, and disseminating research and scholarship

- maintaining several online channels for resource sharing and communication, including a website, listservs, and social media outlets

The National Resource Center is the trusted expert, internationally recognized leader, and clearinghouse for scholarship, policy, and best practice for all postsecondary student transitions.

Institutional Home

The National Resource Center is located at the University of South Carolina's (USC) flagship campus in Columbia. Chartered in 1801, USC Columbia's mission is twofold: to establish and maintain excellence in its student population, faculty, academic programs, living and learning environment, technological infrastructure, library resources, research and scholarship, public and private support and endowment; and to enhance the industrial, economic, and cultural potential of the state. The Columbia campus offers 324 degree programs through its 15 degree-granting colleges and schools. In fiscal year 2023, faculty generated $243.9 million in funding for research, outreach and training programs. USC is among the top tier of universities receiving Research and Community Engagement designations from the Carnegie Foundation.

CONTENTS

PART 1:
BUILDING A CASE FOR A REIMAGINING OF TRANSITIONS

PART 2:
OUTLINING A NEW THEORETICAL POINT OF VIEW ON TRANSITIONS

PREFACE

The eighth and concluding chapter of this book begins with a simple statement: *This book is a snapshot in time.*

And that is true. This book represents the culmination of discussions, presentations, conference papers, more discussions, rejected article submissions, more discussions, research teams, and some better news on the article submission front that started back in 2017. As anyone who has taken part in the "academic hustle" can attest, the process of working with an idea, refining it, and constructing a compelling argument that allows it to see the light of day can be a bit of a rollercoaster ride with many highs and lows—and, if it's a good one, maybe a few loops and corkscrews.

Yet, this book is not a snapshot of the timeframe that encompasses *that* rollercoaster ride. It's a snapshot of the one that followed. Dallin was lamenting his frustration to Jennifer Keup, his friend and colleague and the executive director of the National Resource Center for The First-Year Experience and Students in Transition, after we had written and submitted several drafts of our initial paper on the topic to academic journals with improvements to the manuscript, but no acceptances for publication. After expressing her empathy for the challenges of publishing a so-called "thought piece," Jennifer, in a clear and direct way, asked, "Why don't you just write the book?"

Truthfully, we had envisioned writing a book, but before embarking on such a work, we felt we needed to have something vetted by our peers, adhering to the hallowed traditions of refereed publication that have served as the bedrock of science since time began. But, since that wasn't working, we really didn't have a good reason for not writing one. So we considered Jennifer's advice and mapped out what a book should, would, and could look like, pieced together a proposal, and submitted it to the National Resource Center for consideration. That's when this snapshot began.

Along with that came a new rollercoaster ride. There have been new highs and lows; unexpected twists and turns; long, nervous inclines (usually occurring just before writing deadlines); points that caused our stomachs to turn a little; and stretches of pure nerdy exhilaration. Without further belaboring the rollercoaster metaphor, it is fair to say our (re)thinking of the rethinking in this book has caused us to challenge and expand our own thinking. Searching for, collecting, reviewing, evaluating, synthesizing, and writing new information naturally forces you to reconsider, scrutinize, and cultivate perspectives. It is our hope that writing this book will be just one of many processes that hold such promise as we continue to grapple with conceptualizations of college student transitions.

So, to situate this snapshot in time, we offer three perspectives in this preface: (a) a discussion of what brings the two of us to this topic, (b) a recognition of our respective positionalities, and (c) the acknowledgement of those who have helped get this book to where it is.

What Brings Us to This Topic? Why Are We Writing This Book?

With this section, it is our intention not to hit readers with a barrage of bona fides about why we are qualified to write this book. Rather, it is more important to know who we are and what brings us to this work. We want to share what it is about our experiences that has led us to this point and why we are interested in the topic of student transitions.

One of the first things each of us did when we started this work was to engage in some reflexive writing about what brought us to the topic of wanting to better understand and clarify the definitions and conceptualizations of college student transitions. What follows is each of our narratives, outlining the factors that brought us to the topic, as well as our motivations for writing the book. We start with Bryce's narrative.

Bryce Bunting: What Brings Me to This Topic? Why Am I Writing This Book?

Looking back on my somewhat circuitous trajectory through higher education, first as a student and then as a professional, the idea of transitions has been a prominent theme in all of my experiences. I've nearly always been in some sort of transition or been thinking about the transitions of others. I transferred twice as an undergraduate. At my last undergraduate institution, I became a peer mentor and learned how to support new college students as they joined our campus community. And each of the professional roles I've had since graduating—orientation professional, administrator in a first-year program, professor, scholar–practitioner—somehow have tied back to the same question: "How can I help people (especially new members of communities) have a positive experience here and learn how to be successful?"

I first began thinking about transitions as a transfer student, although I wouldn't have used the term transition then. I had left a small, private liberal arts college for a large, public research university. After just a few weeks at my new university, I found myself feeling angry, frustrated, discouraged, and becoming increasingly cynical about the higher education enterprise. I wondered why I was so miserable and felt so disconnected. For probably the first time ever, I consciously reflected on why transitions lead some to flourish but others to flounder.

At my first institution (Mars Hill College, now Mars Hill University), I was a student–athlete and had a built-in community waiting for me when I arrived. I quickly formed relationships and found meaning in being part of a team and representing my school. Keeping a daily journal allowed me to regularly reflect on how I was growing and who I was becoming. I was also a student athletics trainer, a position that provided nearly daily opportunities to integrate my academic and social experiences; in the training room, I could apply what I was learning in my classes while spending time with people I considered friends.

In short, I felt part of my communities, was able to contribute to and participate in meaningful ways, and because I was reflecting each day in my journal, I could see myself growing. I loved it there, and I felt like people loved having me there.

Leaving Mars Hill College was hard, and I struggled with the decision for months. I felt like I was severing ties with friends, giving up my identity as an athlete, and losing membership in two communities I loved—my soccer team and my athletics training friends and mentors. However, my academic interests had shifted, and the tuition at a small liberal arts school was expensive.

So, arriving at the University of Utah—a large, public research institution—was jarring. I was living at home again, which felt like backward progress. I wasn't involved on campus. I had no friends in my classes and felt unknown to my professors. I drove to campus in the morning for class, went to the library to study after class, left the library for work, then returned home and repeated the pattern the next day. Before the start of that semester, I think I took a campus tour of some kind and met with an academic advisor to map out a graduation plan. However, I always felt isolated, like an outsider watching everyone else have a great time. Not surprisingly, I transferred again.

After a year at my third stop—Brigham Young University, a large, faith-based undergraduate research institution—I was encouraged to apply to be a peer mentor in the university's Office of First-Year Experience.

The experience of becoming a peer mentor would be the single most impactful thing to happen to me. In this role, I received training and mentoring that provided a new, more critical lens through which to make sense of my own transition experiences. I found a community of peers fully committed to their own learning and to helping other students become good learners, and I became immersed in work that connected me with campus resources, faculty members, and leadership opportunities. Additionally, I had a front-row seat for the transition experiences of the students I was assigned to mentor, and then structured opportunities to reflect on and dialogue about how student development and learning theory could be applied to help those students succeed. Peer mentoring was like a paid apprenticeship, and it opened the door for my eventual work as a higher education professional and scholar.

When I reflect on key experiences since then, a similar pattern emerges. For me, transitions presented opportunities, not just for developing new knowledge or skills, but to be transformed and have my identity (re)shaped by the experiences of joining a new community and becoming a full-fledged member of that community. I believe deeply and personally that transitions have transformative potential because, quite simply, it happened to me. I also experienced (on a relatively small scale and not at all to the degree many students do) the pain and discomfort of a "failed transition," one in which I felt lost and never really connected with my campus community.

Dallin Young: What Brings Me to This Topic? Why Am I Writing This Book?

For me, the seeds for the ideas that have sprouted and flowered while writing this book were planted before I ever became a student affairs professional, even before I knew there was such a thing. In high school, I was fortunate to have opportunities to take concurrent enrollment classes and earn credits through nearby Snow College. Being a precocious and somewhat achievement-oriented young person, I took advantage of as many of these opportunities as I could, even enrolling in a full load of courses the summer between my junior and senior years of high school. When I arrived at Utah State University as a first-year student, I entered with junior class standing because of my accumulated Snow College and AP credits.

Scheduling my first quarter was straightforward. I took two first-year seminars, one a general university-wide student success course and the other an introduction and orientation to the college of engineering. After filling in the rest of my schedule with a math class, a drafting class, and the first class in the required biology sequence for my declared major—pre-biological and agricultural engineering—I had it all figured out.

The second quarter was a bit rockier, however. Because I had essentially taken all the typical general education courses, it made the most sense to focus on the required engineering courses, which meant I would take ENGR 200, or Engineering Mechanics: Statics. This is where the first problem presented itself. Typically, students took ENGR 200 alongside a Linear Algebra course during their second or early third years, but my sequence was out of whack, as I was still two quarters away from Linear Algebra. So for my ENGR 200 experience, I had to solve systems of equations by hand while the rest of the class performed magic on their calculators.

Because I was younger than everyone else taking the class and had a good group of friends between my roommates and classmates from the previous term, I made no friends and joined no study groups from the class and therefore had no idea there was a much easier way to solve these equations. So, despite a pretty good showing in the balsa wood bridge-building competition, I got a D in the course (sorry, Mom).

Of course, I did not think about this as an issue related to my transition at the time. I had no framework, language, or concepts to lean on to help understand or describe my experience. In fact, only recently have I started to think about how my transition experiences as an undergraduate have shaped my professional interests. Those experiences in which I felt like I belonged, namely my roles in student leadership as a resident assistant and through the Residence Hall Student Association, became the constants throughout my experience.

Sometime after my second year, I had a moment of reflection, deciding I was not happy with becoming an engineer (I had switched over to electrical engineering by then) and feeling I would not be happy if I were doing that 20 years later. Conversely, and not long after, I walked past the office of a housing administrator whom I had gotten to know as a student leader and thought, "If I had that kind of job in 20 years, I would feel good about it."

Fast forward those 20 years, and here I am, writing about these experiences. What I have presented does not yet explain what brings my attention to transitions or why I felt the need to write this book, however. The answer to those questions comes from my experiences (a) as a housing professional working in first-year communities, (b) as an instructor in a first-year seminar, and (c) as a researcher focused on supporting students in transition.

Before my life as a researcher and faculty member, I saw myself as a "housing guy," but even then, I was concerned about how to make the residential experience as meaningful a learning opportunity for students as any of the rest of the collegiate experience. As an area coordinator for the First-Year Community at California College of the Arts (CCA), I saw young and talented artists looking for ways to get their work shown. One afternoon, I received a postcard from a student inviting me to their senior gallery show. I asked my two colleagues with whom I shared a workspace, both of them CCA graduates, where students learned to curate their own shows. Did they take a class on it? Did they have opportunities to practice it?

It turned out that the first show the students were required to put on was also the last one: the senior show. So, I decided to take what little space we had in the building to create a small gallery dedicated to first-year student art. Students could gain practice in thinking about what art to display and how to present it to the public.

Throughout my role as a housing guy, I was making choices akin to those of a first-year experience professional without yet adopting that identity. After CCA, I moved east to take a job as a residence life coordinator over two residence halls in a complex referred to as "the Towers" at the University of South Carolina (USC), where I was excited to work in what was then called a "freshman community." I was fortunate enough to be on a committee to reimagine and strengthen an early form of what is now widely known as a residential curriculum for first-year students, to participate in a rudimentary form of early alert for the students in housing, and to become a University 101 first-year seminar course instructor.

It was while working with students in all these ways that I started thinking more explicitly about their transition. So many students in the Towers at USC were looking to find a place to fit in, to explore their growing independence, to figure out what it meant to be a student at a university, and who they wanted to be. While I was trying to be the best housing guy for these students, I started to become a student of transitions. I even used Schlossberg's transitions theory to put together a training module for my resident advisors to get them to think about how they could help support students using the 4 'S's: Self, Strategy, Support, and Situation (All these years later, and I can still do that from memory!).

Later, after earning a doctorate to pursue a career as a researcher and (hopefully) a professor, I took a position directing research activities at the National Resource Center for The First-Year Experience and Students in Transition, and again I was fortunate to be an instructor for the University 101 course at USC. At one point, students in my three-hour credit-bearing class that counted toward their academic credential asked me why I was assigning more challenging work and requiring more hours of service from them than their friends in other sections of the course. They even went to RateMyProfessor.com to warn other students about being in my class for taking it too seriously!

Looking for insight, I brought up these reactions to a couple of my co-workers who were also engaged with first-year students. One of my colleagues, who was perennially nominated for the Award for Outstanding Teaching in U101, faced something similar every semester: Students were upset that he expected more from them than their friends were experiencing in other sections. The other colleague, who was teaching sections of English 101 at the same time, required students to do a lot more than either of us did, for the same three graded credit hours. Moreover, she shared that her students did not complain about being asked to do a lot of writing.

I started to wonder why that was: "What is it about these courses and students' expectations that lead to these complaints?" Later, I heard a colleague, who is a philosophy professor, share the idea that "a complaint is a cry for meaning." So, what was the meaning the students in my U101 classes were looking for that I was not communicating when I was asking them to do the things I had read about as important forms of academic engagement?

Further rumblings in my mind around the notions of transitions were inspired by two experiences happening within short succession of each other. The first came during a meeting of the Association for the Study of Higher Education. The session focused on studies of student transitions, and David Vacchi, one of the participants, shared some work he was doing on student transitions for veterans. On my way out of the session, I stopped to tell David how much I enjoyed hearing his findings, including his assertion that we needed to rethink transitions for student veterans.

"Schlossberg doesn't work for student veterans," he shared. "We need a new transition theory."

In 2014, he and Joseph Berger explored and expounded on that idea in a paper. Not long after that, Jennifer Keup, the executive director of the National Resource Center, stopped by my office and, after sharing some frustration with a manuscript she was reviewing, said: "The theoretical framework [on transitions] in this paper just wasn't doing anything for them. … We need to come up with a new transitions theory!"

Well, here we are.

Positioning Ourselves in Our Work

As you read through our personal narratives, you may have had similar experiences, held comparable ideas, and wondered about practice like we did. It is highly likely you have other reasons for caring about student transitions, based on your own experiences and background. You might also have known someone whose transition story is very different from your own, and recognize it is every bit as valid a perspective on the college student experience.

Because of this, we want to be very clear and open about who we are and how that informs our perspective. To that end, we have each crafted a short positionality statement that orients us socially in the conversation. These statements are not offered as apologies for who we are or as excuses for any oversights on our part, but rather as introductions to our subjectivities. Writing these early in our process was intentional, as we wanted to ensure we were also aware of how our subjectivities informed our choices while we searched, interrogated, analyzed, synthesized, and reorganized the theoretical bricolage we present in this book.

Bryce Bunting's Positionality

It is important to recognize my biases and privilege. I am a White, college-educated male, born to White, college-educated parents. Though I have experienced some degree of challenge through personal experiences with transition, I have largely been part of systems and institutions designed for people like me. I have never faced any degree of systematic oppression or exclusion at any point in my life. Thus, while I can listen to the stories of others (both personal narratives as well as more formal research narratives) to understand and empathize with what it might be like to experience transitions from a position of marginality, I cannot ever really understand that experience. Consequently, I will always be, to some degree or another, blind to the experiences of large groups of the higher education population.

Dallin Young's Positionality

I am an abled, White, heterosexual, cisgender male who grew up in rural central Utah. I was raised in a family where education was important, and around me were symbols and messages that higher education was important. All of my parental figures had received post-secondary education, including my mother, who returned to college to complete her bachelor's degree while she was raising three boys and giving birth to a fourth. I was raised in the Church of Jesus Christ of Latter-Day Saints faith tradition, which provided a foundation for many of my principles of ethics, justice, and care.

My college experience largely took place in the 1990s and was marked by a number of transitions: concurrent enrollment, traditional first-year enrollment at a large state university, stopping out for two years, returning after the break, changing majors, academic probation, and withdrawal and readmission. In addition, my educational experience involves traditional student affairs preparation at both the master's and doctoral level with training on the history of higher education and student affairs administration, student development theory, organizational theory, and administrative practices.

These experiences form powerful frames that organize, shape, and inform my understanding of the social world. Yet, understanding them also provides a base from which I can recognize and empathize with others. I am committed to processes of learning so that I can become more aware of how my positions dictate how I perceive and present in the world.

Acknowledgements

This book would not have been possible without the contributions of others who have supported us. We are grateful to those who gave helpful feedback on early drafts of the initial work that led to this book, including Harrison Kleiner, Christina Yao, Matt

Sanders, Rachel Smith, Jean Henscheid, and John Gardner. Thanks to Ka'lah Paige, who was instrumental in helping us organize and corral all the references. We're grateful to the members of the transitions theory systematic review research team who helped us comb through so many journal articles: Alana Hadley Long, Aaron George, Mark Jestel, Kevin Crawford, and Jessica Moore. We would like to thank the leadership team at the National Resource Center: Jennifer Keup, Rico Reed, and Lauren Writer, who not only gave us the opportunity to publish our work but provided crucial developmental feedback on our proposal that shaped the book's direction. We're grateful to the reviewers for their thoughtful, insightful, and challenging feedback. This book would not be as good as it (hopefully) is without your perspectives. We're especially grateful to Stephanie McFerrin who undertook the herculean task of moving mountains to expedite the design and production of this book.

We would also like to acknowledge our friends, families, students, and colleagues who have had to hear us talk about this work in some form or fashion for the past year. Thank you for your patience, grace, and contributions. We could not have done it without your support.

Onward ...

It is with hopeful audacity and optimistic longing that this book came to life. One of the most audacious choices we made involves its tone. After writing the first chapter (not Chapter 1, by the way), we had a long conversation about how we should communicate these ideas in a way that would honor their importance and demonstrate the depth of study that we undertook to arrive at these conclusions, while also remaining accessible and holding your attention. We hope you find the results at least somewhat entertaining and insightful.

Thus, what follows is an invitation to reimagine college student transitions. We do not think much reimagining will be required to see our descriptions of the theory–practice in the lives of students and higher educators, however. While not everyone will agree with the conclusions we have come to, we hope that our critics will at least find these ideas provocative and will spark a conversation on what it means for students to transition to higher education. All we ask is that you give these ideas a chance.

PART 1:
BUILDING A CASE FOR A REIMAGINING OF TRANSITIONS

Chapter 1 | Why Rethinking Transitions Matters

Why a rethinking and reimagining of college student transitions? One of the hallmarks of a field focused on education and learning—particularly one with the audacity to label itself higher education—is a willingness to regularly reflect on the field's current state and identify needed refinements. An examination of the story of "transition work" in higher education highlights that (a) scholars and practitioners have engaged in a somewhat consistent and ongoing pattern of reflective reformation and (b) these reimaginings have helped move the thinking and practice about college transitions forward in important ways.

Indeed, the modern movement associated with supporting college transitions grew out of a critical examination of the "sink-or-swim" attitude toward student success in higher education that had prevailed up to that point. Beginning in the 1960s, institutions started to prioritize accessibility, opening their doors to a broader segment of the American population, one that included older students, low-income students, and students from a variety of minoritized populations. Over the ensuing decades, however, pressures for accountability in higher education made institutions attend to the fact that accessibility was not just about admitting a more diverse student population. Institutions needed to find better ways to help students be successful once they arrived on campus. Consequently, in the 1980s and 1990s formalized efforts to study and better understand college transitions began in earnest, with a particular focus on the first year.

Since then, a proliferation of evidence suggests student success is dependent not only on what happens in the first year, but on a host of other transition experiences, including the sophomore year experience, the senior year capstone experience, the transfer student experience, the experiences of "swirling" students, and the transition from college to career. Not to be outdone, a growing chorus of voices have joined in to claim that "the third year is crucial and doesn't get the respect it deserves" (Mintz, 2019).

As we will discuss in greater depth in Chapter 2, researchers and practitioners have defined transitions in a variety of ways. Some describe transitions as simply *movement* from one setting or phase to another, with an accompanying need to *adjust* to or find *stability* in an unfamiliar environment. Others see college transitions through a slightly more developmental lens, placing an emphasis on helping students acquire new skills and perspectives deemed essential for success in their new circumstances.

While we see practical value in the perspectives offered by these common conceptualizations of college transitions, we argue that transitions are not just opportunities to induct students into a new setting or help them develop new skills and abilities. Instead, we will argue throughout this book that transitions hold transformative potential and are opportunities to support students in a more fundamental, pervasive, and ongoing kind of *becoming*.

Accordingly, we think about transitions as the process by which students become full and contributing participants in their various communities—their classrooms, their disciplines, their residential environments, and the campus at large. Similarly, we assert that institutions are most effective in supporting student transitions when they do more than just "orient" students and, instead, prioritize giving students access to the experiences, tools, conversations, and relationships that offer authentic membership in the community. Epitomizing this membership are opportunities for students to engage with others— faculty, peers, administrators, and anyone else actively involved in the intellectual life of the university—as full participants in meaningful activities that matter both to the student and to the institution.

Why This Book? Why Now?

This book aims to deepen understanding of *why* attending to transitions—all the various transitions that make up the college experience—will be even more essential in coming years. More importantly, it provides guidance for *how* we can better define, describe, analyze, and support transitions in ways that acknowledge the shifting higher education landscape and the increasingly diverse students on our campuses.

Let us be clear: Higher education has benefitted tremendously from the important theories on college transitions developed over the past 50 years. A few of these include foundational works such as Tinto's theory of academic and social integration, Schlossberg's transition model, Weidman's model of undergraduate socialization, Laanan's model of transfer capital, Attinasi's description of the importance of "getting in" for Mexican

Americans during their first year, and Schooler's Native American transition theory. Additionally, thought leaders such as Betsy Barefoot, John Gardner, Sylvia Hurtado, George Kuh, Ernest Pascarella, Terrell Strayhorn, and Patrick Terenzini, among many others, provided critical foundational understanding that has illuminated the challenges and developmental needs of students in transition.

However, as Upcraft et al. (2005) argued nearly 20 years ago, colleges and universities must be "willing to make major changes in their approach to learning if they [are] to serve students in the 1990s and beyond" (p. 1). In concert with these researchers, we argue that "major changes" similarly are required in our current thinking and theorizing about transitions if we are to support *today's* college students in the current higher education landscape. Ultimately, the corpus of theoretical frameworks commonly used to make sense of the phenomenon of college transitions has important gaps that have largely gone unacknowledged by researchers and practitioners alike. As we will work to demonstrate, traditional approaches to college transitions fall short in several ways:

- they do not acknowledge the pervasive and ongoing nature of college transitions;

- they are inadequate for promoting inclusion and belonging for an increasingly diverse student population;

- they tend to conceptualize transitions as merely individual or personal concerns; and

- they fail to leverage the potential for transformation and becoming in transitions.

As a way of orienting the reader to our main critiques of the current theoretical landscape related to college transitions, we will briefly discuss these key gaps here.

The Ongoing Nature of Transitions

Much of the scholarship and practice focused on college transitions is grounded in paradigms of transition framed as induction, movement, adjustment, or development (Gale & Parker, 2014), placing a focus either on helping students adjust during specified periods of time or helping them successfully complete particular developmental tasks. However, college transitions are more than just episodic, time-bound punctuations that begin and end in concert with the whims of the registrar and their calendar. In fact, such a view risks arbitrarily elevating some transitions while minimizing others. Instead, we call for a more nuanced understanding of the college experience as a protracted series of transitions that flow into, out of, and through one another. From this perspective, transition is not an isolated event occurring at a small number of pre-determined points in a student's college experience. Rather, students experience a series of interconnected and ongoing transitions that open the door for a process of continual learning and becoming (more on this in a moment). Indeed, we assert that transitions are inseparable from learning, participation, and becoming.

Consequently, we often conceptualize transitions as problems we need to solve, rather than as educative—or even essential—learning opportunities that facilitate deep and meaningful learning. Indeed, Tobbell & O'Donnell (2005) described transitions as natural aspects of engaging in new communities and that "to understand [them] as a problem is to reify and separate knowledge from context" (p. 10). Similarly, student support units frequently characterize their work using phrases such as "removing challenges," "easing transitions," and "accommodating students," suggesting transitions require an approach separate from our planned learning processes.

In short, we often view transitions as something to "get through" so students can return to the relative calm of the "normal" college experience and continue with the process of real learning. We argue, instead, for a reconceptualization of transitions—one that recognizes that learning, transition, and navigating unfamiliarity are all pathways to the deep and lasting learning we promise students they will experience when they arrive on our campuses.

Transitions as Pathways to Inclusion and Belonging for Today's Students

While challenges in transition can be the source of important learning, the fact remains that, for historically minoritized students, we have too frequently created or tolerated systemic challenges that hold no educative value. Further, though traditional transition theory and frameworks provided critical early understanding of the importance of attending to the needs and challenges of students in transition, these frameworks grew out of a time when higher ed institutions' primary focus was on educating a relatively homogenous group of Americans. More simply, 20th century theoretical frameworks generally describe what the college transition looked like for a largely White, financially stable, and otherwise privileged population of students. This has tremendous implications for current efforts to advance diversity, equity, and inclusion across college campuses.

The reality is that the search for innovations that improve educational quality and equity and support success for all students is partly dependent on the theoretical seedbeds from which innovations spring. Though persistence and retention rates have improved slightly overall, ultimately, too many students still stop out, and concerns regarding equity gaps across various demographic groups still exist (National Student Clearinghouse Research Center, 2022). Thus, we still have a great deal of work to do. Consequently, any conversation about transition is inherently one about access, equity, inclusion, and belonging. When institutions fail to support students in transition, they perpetuate inequities and maintain the status quo.

Further, the traditional approaches to supporting transition described previously in this chapter often inadvertently push students to the margins by "involving [them] in the [campus] community in some ways while keeping them at arm's length in others" (O'Donnell & Tobbell, 2007, pp. 317–318). We find it somewhat ironic that a significant degree of institutional efforts to orient, welcome, and support students in transition rely on a model that essentially separates students from the larger campus community, then engages them in practices and activities that are not part of the practice of that broader community.

To help illustrate this problem, consider a familiar driving metaphor. Nearly every reader has used an on-ramp to transition from a surface street onto a freeway or expressway. This simple innovation allows a driver to enter the freeway's ongoing high-speed traffic flow in a somewhat gradual, safe, and natural way. Of course, there can still be challenges in merging from the ramp to a formal traffic lane and increasing your speed to integrate with the flow of traffic, but the on-ramp provides a relatively natural method of doing so.

In contrast, imagine the frustration, confusion, and danger that would ensue if your on-ramp ended with a 90-degree turn onto what is essentially a different road just before the intersection point with the freeway. While the on-ramp might have allowed you to observe the speed and direction you would need to adopt to merge onto the freeway, it hasn't actually placed you on an effective trajectory to allow you to become part of the ongoing flow of traffic.

To show what we mean here and why it is important, we point to a common refrain in the literature about programs that support sophomore student success. The critique frequently follows this pattern: Students who return for their second year of college are confronted with the challenges that come with attendance, but as the institution turns its attention to a new group of incoming first-year students, sophomore students report feeling abandoned. The supports they grew accustomed to are no longer in place, thereby simply postponing their real transition to the second year (Hartman & Young, 2021; Schaller, 2010; Schreiner, 2018; Skipper, 2019; Young et al., 2015). Frequently, we have heard this phenomenon informally referred to as the first-year experience simply "moving the cliff" of retention from the first to the second year. Therefore, as transition support was only concerned with moving students from one sense of stability to a new one (i.e., from pre-arrival, through arrival and adjustment at college, to stability by the conclusion of the first year), a sense of abandonment or the experience of "barely surviving" (Schreiner, 2018, p. 9) indicates the interventions offered in the first year were situated in that place and time and did not provide durable or ongoing benefits to the students who received them.

We do not love the term "college onboarding," but, for simplicity's sake, if the way we "onboard" students to new experiences in college occurs on a distinctly different road and requires distinctly different skills and practices, students' transition onto the "main road" (e.g., after their first-year experience) may involve some damaged fenders.

All of this highlights the need to differentiate between what we term *productive peripherality* and *miseducative marginalization*. Productive peripherality in college transitions provides an appropriate degree of scaffolding and safety as students navigate the unfamiliarity and risk that come with transitions. In contrast, miseducative marginalization is what we might describe as "overly protective," in that it provides so much insulation and separation from the broader campus community that students are denied access to the people, practices, conversations, and resources (the on-ramp as it were) essential to helping them become fully participating members of their campus community. This marginalization is particularly problematic for first-generation students and students with minoritized identities because it further obscures the hidden curriculum of higher education and serves as another barrier to the forms of participation most likely to lead to full membership in the campus community. Navigating this tension between peripherality and marginalization is a key consideration for anyone interested in supporting students in transition.

Transitions Are Not Individual Endeavors

Though transitions involve learning about oneself, discovering new abilities, developing pride in one's competence, and exploring a new *possible self* (Markus & Nurius, 1986), they are not merely individual matters. Transitions intersect with issues of community, membership, and access.

The past few decades of research have provided nearly indisputable evidence of the necessity of fostering belonging among college students. Students are more likely to persist, be retained, and thrive when they feel a sense of belonging in their community (e.g., Means & Pyne, 2017; Nunn, 2021; Silver, 2020; Strayhorn, 2018) and are offered opportunities for meaningful participation and involvement with others on their campus (e.g., Astin, 1984; O'Donnell & Tobbell, 2007; Quaye et al., 2019; Vetter et al., 2019).

However, much of the scholarship on college transitions narrowly defines *community* as the social ties that develop in traditional transition programs (e.g., new-student orientation, first-year learning communities), in first-year seminar courses, or through students' informal social interactions with peers. A sense of belonging in a social community is just one of a variety of ways in which students can experience the benefits of community during times of transition. Our hope is to expand readers' conception of this term beyond traditional notions of social community (Nunn, 2021) to a more inclusive and encompassing view of the variety of communities that students could connect with during transitions. Ultimately, those interested in student transitions have an obligation to collaborate with colleagues on our campuses to design spaces that offer varied forms of community and belonging to students from a diverse range of backgrounds and identities.

We hope this book and its focus on community and relationships will spur productive conversations about the role of community in transitions; what "counts" as community; how to support students in making new community connections while honoring ties to prior communities (particularly familial and cultural); and how *joining* a community might be different from *participating* in that community.

Transitions as Transformation and Becoming

This brings us to the main premise of our book and our major critique of existing approaches to college transitions. As we have alluded to already, transitions are not just momentary disruptions in the college experience requiring students to adjust to a new way of doing things. Further, transitions are more than the first few weeks of a new "phase" in the lifespan of a student—for example, the beginning of the second year, the first semester after declaring a major, or the six months a student on academic suspension might be required to spend away from school.

Transitions are times of potential transformation.

To realize this potential, however, those of us charged with researching and supporting these transitions need a new theoretical lens to guide our work.

We chose to write this book because we have seen and experienced how transitions can facilitate becoming. You likely have, too. You probably know college students who, across their various transitions, have not just achieved specific aims or learning outcomes identified by their institution, but have experienced a more comprehensive and durable kind of becoming that has impacted their lives well beyond the classroom. We have also discovered evidence of this transformative potential scattered across the research landscape (e.g., Bunting & Williams, 2017; Gorgorió, 2002; Sanders, 2018; Yanchar et al., 2013). In the end, our hope is to convince readers that the various transitions making up the college experience can, together, prepare students for future personal challenge and change, as well as prepare them to be full participants in future communities—their homes, cities, jobs, and social circles. From this new philosophical ground, with its elevated perspective, we can engage in a new kind of conversation about transitions, one focused on supporting students as they navigate the challenges of transitions, while also leveraging the potential for transformation and becoming that are inherent in these same challenges. So, as we have articulated already, transitions are not problems or crises, but times of potential transformation.

Transitions: A New Theoretical Framework

Clearly, the writing of this book and exploration of these questions make for an ambitious undertaking. However, our review of the literature on transitions has ultimately left us feeling what we've come to describe as *optimistic longing*.

Yes, there are gaps in current theorizing, and we long for theory that helps better describe the experience of an increasingly diverse population of college students. However, we feel optimistic about the potential for a reconceptualization of transitions in higher education because of what we see happening in pockets of innovation around the world, including good work by our colleagues in South Africa, Australasia, and Europe, as well as here in the United States. On these campuses, we see canny and thoughtful practitioners rethinking practices and programs, along with innovative interventions that support diverse students in transition and move beyond simplistic goals of induction toward transformation and becoming. We will highlight examples of approaches we have labeled as "becomingist" throughout the book.

Additionally, clusters of theories scattered across the literature point to the transformative potential of college transitions and suggest that other practitioners feel a resonance with the perspective of transitions as becoming. Accordingly, we have attempted to outline the foundations of a reconceptualized theoretical framework for student transitions in higher education based on previous theoretical work, including situated learning and legitimate peripheral participation in communities of practice (Lave & Wenger, 1991; Wenger, 1998) and transitions as "becoming" (Ecclestone et al., 2010; Hamshire & Jack, 2016; Gale & Parker, 2014; Sanders, 2018). Thus, our current work might be best described as *theoretical bricolage* (Kincheloe, 2011), in that we have taken a critical and rigorous approach to creating a new theoretical conceptualization of transitions by weaving together key elements and perspectives of existing theoretical models of college transition. Together, these diverse but conceptually coherent "bricks" come together to provide a new, more critical, and more practical lens for pursuing future avenues of inquiry and evaluation of practice related to how we support college transitions.

Most importantly, our hope in writing this book is to provide new tools—both theoretical and practical—for improving the learning of students across the many transitions that make up the college experience. Moreover, we advocate rethinking transitions in order to move beyond approaches that perpetuate gaps or narrowly focus on transitional events that are most convenient to the institution. To that end, we are more concerned with the underlying features of student transitions that guide institutional responses than we are about specific programmatic approaches that lend themselves to a one-size-fits-all approach to transitions. The field of higher education has fallen short by naively defining transitions as periodic and isolated elements of college. This assumption has led to the false belief that we can design uniform programs or tactics to support students in transition by merely familiarizing them with policies, practices, resources, and expectations. Doing so limits the transformative potential of transitions and fails to acknowledge the reality that today's students take a variety of paths as they navigate their personal transitions. In rethinking the ways we approach transitions, we have a chance to close these gaps and help students leverage their opportunities for becoming inherent in the college experience.

Our book provides guidance on how to balance challenge and support by introducing three key *modes of transition*: community, participation, and becoming. We have grounded our thinking about these modes and their role in transitions in the assumption that becoming a college student is not altogether different from the experience of a novice entering any new community of practice (Lave & Wenger, 1991; Wenger, 1998). Specifically, entering a new community involves a shift from peripheral forms of participation toward increasingly advanced forms of participation with the community's more experienced members. More succinctly, new students become experienced learners as they both acquire the knowledge and skills needed to navigate their various communities and, more importantly, participate in these communities in ways that signal membership and offer significant opportunities to contribute to the work of the institution. Even more simply, students learn to do college by *doing* college, albeit with a particular set of supports, experiences, and opportunities. This book is our attempt to convince practitioners and thought leaders of the importance of attending to issues of community, participation, and becoming when it comes to these transition experiences.

Who Is This Book For?

While we hope this book makes it into the hands of a wide variety of folks with an interest in student transitions, we have envisioned a couple of primary audiences for our work. First are higher education practitioners who seek to understand and improve the experiences of students in transition. This group includes transition program personnel, particularly those in decision-making positions for the design and execution of programs, administrators responsible for student success on campus, and researchers with an interest in studying the experiences of students in transition.

More broadly, we hope this book will hold appeal and utility for a group of readers we have termed "thought leaders." While this terminology might be both grandiose and vague, it helped us focus on people we think will serve as principal consumers of the work. Perhaps the primary group of thought leaders who form the audience for the book are higher education and student affairs graduate program faculty, particularly those who teach courses on student development theory, student success, or college student environments. These faculty are critical to sharing and shaping the prevailing professional perspectives in the field, and their power and influence cannot be overestimated. Indeed, the theories, models, frameworks, and philosophical orientations faculty choose to highlight and make visible to graduate students will shape the thinking and practice of the field immeasurably.

The second group of important thought leaders are transition program directors. These individuals set the agenda for the day-to-day practice of the programs they administer. Having these thought leaders adopt the principles and orientation emphasized in the book will both improve practice and influence the thinking and practice of the colleagues with whom they work, including the graduate students they supervise in practicum and internship experiences. Consequently, we have labored to write a volume that blends theoretical reconceptualization with plenty of discussion of the practical application of those ideas.

Ultimately, supporting students in transition is not about a single person, program, or policy. Rather, it hinges on institutions' ability to create communities that (a) offer students belonging (Nunn, 2021) and (b) invite not just passive "engagement" via observation and proximity, but also invite (or even require) students to join the campus community by actively contributing to its practices. Therefore, really, this book is for anyone with a stake in supporting transitions.

How Is This Book Structured?

In keeping with the overarching goal of providing a reconceptualization of college student transitions to inform both scholarship and practice, we have organized the book around a core set of questions, each of which is explored in a distinct section:

- (Part 1) Where are the gaps in current approaches to college transitions? Why do we need a reimagined theoretical foundation?

- (Part 2) What are the essential components or modes of an approach to understanding supporting transitions as a process of becoming?

- (Part 3) How can this reconceptualization be applied in practical ways across a variety of transitions in higher education? What are the implications for practice, policy, and research?

- (Part 4) What is the path forward? How might this model need to be revised or expanded?

These questions provided general guidance as we conceptualized the book, and framed the organization and content of the chapters that outline the basis and the consequences of our arguments.

In this opening chapter, we have attempted to make a case for the need for new transition theory and why now is the right time to begin articulating its reconceptualization. In Chapter 2, we provide an integrative overview of the landscape on research and scholarly practice literature on transitions by identifying and critiquing general ways that transitions are defined in higher education literature. We then introduce a new conceptualization and definition of "transition as becoming."

Part 2 of the book focuses on outlining a new theoretical point of view on transitions. In Chapter 3, we review the fundamental aspects of *situated learning, legitimate peripheral participation* (Lave & Wenger, 1991), and *transition as becoming* (Gale & Parker, 2014) as both a foundation for new thinking of transition theory as well as a conceptual bridge between current approaches to supporting transitions and the new framework outlined in this book. In Chapter 4, we introduce three main "modes" of transition—community, participation, and becoming—and make the case for why a focus on these elements of transitions is so important. These modes are at the core of the new theoretical framework described in the book and are the central focus of the chapters that follow.

Part 3 expands our discussion of the practical application of this theoretical framework. In service of our aim to maximize the book's practical utility, Chapter 5 is devoted to a discussion of how these *modes of transition* can guide the process of designing, implementing, and assessing transition programs and initiatives. In Chapter 6, we describe the dynamic interplay between these three modes of transition and provide more examples of practices that leverage these modes and illustrate the power of *community, participation,* and *becoming.* Chapter 7 is devoted to a discussion of key implications of the theory for institutional leaders. These include recommendations for how campus leaders can apply this framework to invisible sites of transition, including gateway courses, developmental education, high-impact practices, and academic probation.

Finally, in Part 4 and Chapter 8, we chart a course forward and offer a concluding integrative overview of our proposed theoretical approach. We then outline needed revisions and improvements to our framework and map out directions and recommendations for future research and inquiry into these ideas.

An Invitation to Readers

Writing a book like this is risky, in that some readers may be hoping to find a one-size-fits-all strategy, intervention, or program to address the challenge of student transitions in a seemingly magical way. Consequently, we want to make clear: Any concrete strategy or example you might encounter in what follows does not suggest this particular strategy or application of our framework will be appropriate for all students or for every institution. Providing sure-fire or guaranteed interventions was never our intent, and readers searching for such treasure will be disappointed.

Instead, what we hope to convince you is that the most high-impact approaches to supporting transitions—those that open the door for transformation—need to attend to the three modes of transition introduced in Chapter 4 (i.e., community, participation, and becoming). Consequently, we encourage readers to take a critical and context-conscious approach to implementing and applying the ideas we present. As authors, we see our role as one of introducing you to a new set of theoretical tools you can deploy and adjust to fit the unique challenges and opportunities of your space. Ultimately, we hope the reconceptualization of transitions outlined in the book provides a new lens through which to think about, make sense of, and support transitions in higher education.

Consequently, we invite you to primarily focus on understanding the modes of transition we have introduced, consider their application in your own practice, then regularly reflect on and discuss with colleagues how these ideas might inform (a) new scholarship on college transitions and (b) the design or redesign of transition programming on your campus. Supporting students in learning and becoming requires an integrated, holistic, and campus-wide approach that engages all stakeholders. These efforts should be responsive to the multiplicity of global, institutional, and historical factors that influence transitions, as well as the local challenges, opportunities, and needs of your students.

To enhance the practicality of the book and its ideas, we conclude each chapter with a short section titled *Crucial Considerations* (see below). Here, we articulate questions we hope will promote reflection, dialogue with colleagues, evaluation of existing practices, and considerations for ongoing contemplation about how what has been presented in the preceding chapter shapes our thinking about supporting transitions.

Ultimately, rethinking transitions involves much more than developing a single premier program or high-impact intervention. Rather, the greater task for those who support students in transition is to find ways to bring together a constellation of research-based and theoretically grounded practices that, together, comprise an environment that offers belonging by actively inviting students to participate in the process of becoming at both the personal and institutional level.

While we hope this book does lead to the development of new programs, interventions, and practices designed to support students in transition, we are just as eager to simply spark dialogue and debate around the ideas we have presented. So, if after reading this first chapter you already have questions, concerns, new wonderings, or sparks of insight—we have done our job. Happy reading! We look forward to the conversations that result.

Crucial Considerations

The following questions can help guide or initiate conversations with key players on your campus and serve as starting points for implementing change:

- What are the current needs, opportunities, and challenges associated with transitions on your campus? Where are you hoping to make changes or refinements?

- What theoretical frameworks are you and your colleagues relying on to guide the transition programming on your campus? How well are these frameworks serving you? Are there ways in which they fall short?

- How might you balance challenge and support during times of transition?

Chapter 2 | What Do We Mean by "Transition"?

The discussion around student transitions is one of interest to such a wide array of people that it might seem self-evident. In fact, our review of the research literature shows that often, transition represents a concept assumed to be understood so widely and so well that it requires no explanation.

That is far from the case, however.

As we discussed in Chapter 1, there is no commonly held understanding of what "transition" means (Ecclestone et al., 2010), although several basic definitions of the term are present in the literature. To many, transition is simply movement: into a new location, a new identity, a new label, a new social relationship. And we may well define it as such. However, while simple movement or arrival or adjustment may appear to be a universal definition of transition, the reality is much more complex, and transition's use in scholarly literature warrants a serious consideration of the topic. As stated in the previous chapter, we contend that in order to respond to contemporary student needs, we need updated models that more accurately describe students' lived experiences.

Before we get too far ahead of ourselves, though, we would like to put a proverbial stake in the ground and outline how we are (currently) thinking about transitions. First, while transitions are frequently precipitated by movement between social and cultural environments, there is more at play. We see the transition experience for students as an active and ongoing practice rather than a singular event. Taylor and Harris-Evans (2018) assert: "Transitioning [is] an active making and unmaking of the 'thing' called 'transition.'" (p. 1259). Students are actively engaging with it, (dis/re)assembling it, (re)arranging it, and (re)defining what it means to them as they move from one state of being to the next. It is important to not only center the student, but to center the student's agency during and throughout the transition.

Throughout the book, we will present a perspective whereby student transition represents becoming members of an academic community through ongoing practice that includes:

- strengthening meaningful connections with others in the community;

- ongoing, authentic participation in the practices of the community, leading to increased awareness of and experience with knowledge, skills, tools, and language, which in turn facilitate further participation; and

- opening up a trajectory of ways of being, doing, and thinking that are congruent with student goals and images of self.

As we lay out our invitation for you to rethink student transitions throughout this and future chapters, we will explain in further detail how we arrived at these perspectives, as well as what they mean.

Mapping the Theoretical Landscape of Transitions in Higher Education

Our purpose for this chapter is to lay the formal foundation for our case for why we even need to rethink and offer a new theoretical view of transitions. To do this, we set out to map the theoretical and conceptual landscape of transitions in the scholarly literature. Our map of the theoretical landscape will entail a cataloging of the types of common conceptualizations of what we call "transition." More importantly, our mapping of the theoretical landscape will serve not only as a review but also a critique of these groups of theoretical descriptions common in the literature on higher education research, practice, and policy.

We have found Gale & Parker's (2014) typology of transitions in higher education useful and informative in assisting us with this task. Through their review of the research literature, the authors identified three main descriptions of transitions: as induction, development, and becoming. Moreover, through our review of transition literature we will build and expand on that typology, teasing "induction" apart into "movement" and "adjustment" and adding transitions as a sociocultural process. For each of these forms of describing of transition, we will present an overview of the way each of these conceptualizations appears in the literature, followed by a critique in which we name and respond to the challenges each perspective presents.

Transitions as Movement, Adjustment, and Stability

Perhaps the most straightforward way transitions are described in the ongoing conversation about college student success is as movement of the student from one educational location or situation to the next (Coertjens et al., 2017; Kyndt et al., 2017; Schaeper, 2020). This includes discussions of the transition from high school to college, the transfer from community college to a four-year university, "pathways" to and through majors, and movement out of college after graduation into the world of work or ongoing education. Colley (2007) refers to these kinds of conceptualizations as "institutional transitions" and points to policymakers' desire to "ensure smooth and successful progression through these transitions" (p. 429).

Conceptualizations of transitions as movement can be seen through many of the responses that have been created or proposed as "transition programs." When movement into, through, and out of college is of primary concern in transitions, the focus shifts to achievement of procedural goals, including retention, credit accumulation, developmental course completion, or successful navigation of institutional policies and procedures (e.g., Giani, 2019; Hatch & Garcia, 2017; Li & Ortagus, 2019; Mokher & Leeds, 2018; O'Shea, 2015; Pike & Robbins, 2020; Sanabria et al., 2020; Wang, 2017; Wang et al., 2019). A prominent example of the policy and practice that arise from this notion of transitions is the rise of dual credit or concurrent enrollment programs designed to allow high school students to earn college credits as they take advanced coursework. A frequently stated rationale for the adoption of these programs is to "ease," "smooth," or "facilitate" the transition to college (e.g., An & Taylor, 2019; Bailey et al., 2002; Duncheon & Relles, 2020; Fowler & Luna, 2009; U.S. Department of Education, 2003). By so doing, students gain "momentum" toward completing requirements that will facilitate their progression toward graduation.

If movement is part of the conceptualization of college students' transitions, it would only make sense that the next step in understanding transitions would have to do with student *adjustment* to the movement. The adjustment period the transition represents is marked by or begins with a "transition point" or a "critical juncture" (Barefoot et al., 2012; Carpenter et al., 2018; Hartman et al., 2021; Park et al., 2022; Sanagavarapu et al., 2019; Smith & Gayles, 2017; Tholen et al., 2022; Young et al., 2017; Young, 2019). Quinn (2010) describes the adjustment period as "a fixed turning point which takes place at a preordained time and in a certain place" (p. 122). As a result, the primary concern in this perspective is helping students adjust to college by assisting them in recognizing and managing stressors and developing coping skills (Ames et al., 2014; Baker & Siryk, 1999; Koo et al., 2021; Lane, 2020; Melendez, 2015; Mettler et al., 2019; Rogerson & Poock, 2013; Speckman, 2016; Taylor et al., 2016).

Researchers have long applied Schlossberg's theory of transition (Schlossberg, 1981; Schlossberg et al., 1995) to describe the internal psychological process of students going through periods of adjustment that come with college transitions. This theory describes an adjustment process wherein people manage intra- and interpersonal assets and liabilities as they move into, through, and out of changes caused by some external event or by an unrealized but anticipated event. Schlossberg's contribution to and impact on the conversation around college student transitions cannot be discounted; indeed, much of the language around transitions in the literature draws on the *moving in, through,* and *out* framing of transitions that comes from her theory. As an example, the National Resource Center for The First-Year Experience and Students in Transition uses this language in its mission statement to "improve student learning and transitions into and through higher education" (National Resource Center, n.d., Mission statement, para 1).

Schlossberg's approach to understanding transitions shares a similar structure with other perspectives on managing transitions, such as Bridges (2004) and Nicholson and West (1995), as well as Hills' (1965) depiction of "transfer shock." In each of these models, transitions have three general phases: encounter, transition, and stability. In the initial phase, students encounter new and unfamiliar psychological, social, and institutional circumstances that require creating and adopting new perspective(s) as they reconsider their sense of self, their view of the world, and their perceived abilities. The next phase requires students to navigate, negotiate, and make meaning of their new situation and is often marked by discomfort, challenge, and ambivalence about their new environment. This period has been referred to as a liminal or betwixt space—a place where "students can be suspended between one place (home) and another (university), resulting in an 'in-between-ness'" (Palmer et al., 2009, p. 38). In the final phase of the transition, students eventually come to a new set of terms with the change they have experienced and enter a normalized state in which they are deemed settled, socialized, or *stabilized* once the transition is complete. This final state is described variously as moving out (Schlossberg, 1981), new beginnings (Bridges, 2004), stabilization (Nicholson & West, 1995), and recovery, relearning, or adjustment (Hills, 1965; Laanan, 2001, 2004).

Naming and Facing the Challenges with Transitions as Movement, Adjustment, and Stability

When transitions are framed as movement, adjustment, and stability, we begin to notice some of the challenges with these long-held and underexamined conceptualizations.

First, there is inconsistency on whether the "transition" is conceptualized as the movement itself or the process of adjustment that comes from movement (or even both). Examples from research literature illustrate the ways in which scholars are operationalizing and sequencing transitions as separate concepts of movement and adjustment, and how transition is framed as one but not the other. For instance, sometimes transition is described as the movement into new spaces *before* the adjustment (e.g., transition = enrollment and arrival at the university with adjustment occurring afterward; see Mettler et al., 2019, p. 39), and other times the transition is the adjustment process after the movement (e.g., transition = adjustment needed after transfer; see Ogilvie & Knight, 2021, p. 296).

Second, as we mentioned earlier, transition programs are typically embedded at "transition points" (Carpenter et al., 2018; Sanagavarapu et al., 2019) or "critical junctures" (Hartman et al., 2021; Park et al., 2022; Smith & Gayles, 2017; Tholen et al., 2022) along the college pathway as students encounter shifts, such as enrollment, arrival, transfer, or changing their academic or social frames of reference. Framing transitions as critical events shapes the nature of the phenomenon and the natural response from the institution. When transitions are seen as critical points, they are often perceived as a crisis, challenge, or gap that must be ameliorated by an induction process to the university's norms, language, and modes of doing and being (Gale & Parker, 2014; Gravett, 2021; Quinn, 2010). This is typically achieved via formal, scripted introductions to resources, procedures, and policies through such practices as academic advising, new student orientation, or first-year seminars (Hatch & Garcia, 2017; Linley, 2017; Xu et al., 2020; Young, 2020).

As such, when transitions are viewed as movement and adjustment, the institution sets the terms of the transition (Gale & Parker, 2014; Quinn, 2010). Yet, it is the student who must manage challenges and develop coping skills as they move in, through, and out of environments, while "educational administrators, policymakers, and advocates set the contexts within which students navigate education systems" (Kitchen et al., 2019, p. 489) throughout the totality of the student's educational experience. When institutions set the terms of transitions, the steps they require from students are frequently reduced to a set of procedures, sequences, and tasks. Gravett (2021) goes further, suggesting that referring to transitions as a "process" positions "transition as a uniform structural process, distinct from the student" (p. 1508). As a result, transitions become features of systems rather than experiences of individuals (Gravett, 2021).

This is illustrated by referring back to the example of dual enrollment initiatives, which are implemented to *ease, smooth,* or *facilitate* the transition to college (e.g., An & Taylor, 2019; Bailey et al., 2002; Duncheon & Relles, 2020; Fowler & Luna, 2009; U.S. Department of Education, 2003). Conceptualizing the accumulation and movement of credits as the concern that requires a policy response locates the transition itself as external to the student and is therefore a process phenomenon situated at the institutional level. Further, this example represents a disconnect between the purposes and design of the "transition program" (i.e., dual enrollment designed to facilitate credit momentum) and the descriptions and theories of transition typically connected to them. As we illustrated earlier, transition theories frequently describe a psychological journey through which a student manages assets and liabilities in supports, situation, self, and strategies (Schlossberg, 1981; Schlossberg et al., 1995). The disconnect, then, is that transition-focused policies and programs are conceptualized as transition as movement, while the student experience is conceptualized as transition as adjustment and stability.

One of the problems with presenting transitions as challenges that must be overcome to enter and successfully engage in institutions of higher education (Ecclestone et al., 2010; Gale & Parker, 2014; Gravett, 2021; Quinn, 2010) is that we fail to view these critical junctures as opportunities for transformation, growth, and becoming. Moreover, we can also fail to communicate this same idea to the students who are experiencing these transitions. Ecclestone (2007) suggests that institutional efforts to smooth out the emotional difficulties associated with transitions imply that people cannot deal with transitions without formalized support and help. Consequently, our focus and preoccupation with these junctures often signal to students that we view them as unprepared or incompetent. This is particularly poignant for students for whom higher education has historically been denied, such as adult learners, part-time students, those from under-resourced backgrounds, and racially minoritized students, among many others. Students from these backgrounds might be seen as lacking sources of capital required to engage and participate in higher education (Gravett, 2021; Nora, 2004; Perna, 2006; Yosso, 2005). As this focus, instantiated by institutional efforts, depicts students who are "vulnerable and lacking in agency" (Gravett, 2021, p. 1508), it sells people short at best, and infantilizes and subjugates them at worst.

With this information, we can start to pull together some of the components that comprise conceptualizations and operationalizations into a table to help us keep track of such things. Table 2.1 outlines some of the key features of transitions conceptualized as movement and those conceptualized as adjustment and stability.

Table 2.1.

Key components of conceptualizations of transitions as movement, adjustment, and stability

Dimension	Transitions as:	
	Movement	**Adjustment and Stability**
Main image or metaphor	Movement of students between educational institutions	Critical moment initiates a psychological process of adjustment into, through, and out of a challenge brought about by change
Institutional role in supporting transitions	Creating policies that facilitate, ease, or smooth movement between institutions (e.g., high school to university)	Creating conditions that afford students the supports needed to adjust toward social and psychological stability
Orientation to student	External: Concerns related to transitions are with policies, systems, and processes in which students participate	Internal: Student must contend with psychological challenges brought about by changes in the environment
Agency	Institution is centered as agentic; transition terms are set by institutional systems, policy, norms	Institution is centered as agentic; critical points in time and environment are institutionally constructed. Students are respondent; they must contend with adjustment and accommodation into institutional setting

Transitions as Development

Another set of conceptualizations, definitions, and descriptions of student transitions have been described by Gale & Parker (2014) as *transitions as development*. From this perspective, transitions are frequently conceptualized as how students interact with and navigate social dynamics such as expectations, norms, roles, and relationships in a process of psychosocial *development*. This framing of transition focuses on a few key issues. First, it is predicated on a common developmental perspective that changes in the social environment (e.g., enrolling in college, transferring to a (different) university, graduation) punctuate a change in psychosocial status with which students must contend. For example, a working adult enrolls at the local community college, where she now must attend to the psychological task of coming to terms with and making meaning of her new identity as a student. She might now be faced with the *developmental* task of answering the question, "What does this mean for me and how I understand and interact with others in the world?"

This might seem similar to depictions of transitions as movement and adjustment; however, the developmentalist perspective presents a couple of key differences. First, in the transitions as adjustment point of view, the main concern is with moving through socioemotional difficulty to arrive at a new status of stability. While growth or change is a potential, yet not necessary, outcome of adjustment and stability transitions, it is a defining feature of the developmental view of transitions. Second, transitions as development are concerned with how the internal world of the student (the psychological part of "psychosocial") interacts with the structural, cultural, and constructed environments (the social part of "psychosocial") the student finds themselves in (McEwen, 2003). Thus, developmental characterizations of transitions point to one or more potential psychosocial issues that students must face during and as a result of a transition to or in college. These might include identity, purpose, norms, expectations, belonging, or psychological sense of community (see Duran et al., 2020; Murdock-Perriera et al., 2019; Oxendine et al., 2020; Pokorny et al., 2017; Rucks-Ahidiana & Bork, 2020; Schaller 2005, 2018; Schreiner et al., 2020a; Tachine et al., 2017; Young, 2016).

A review of common developmental tasks frequently associated with students at different points in their undergraduate pathways helps illustrate how conceptualizations of transition of development show up in scholarly literature. The objectives for first-year students most frequently identified by institutions participating in the 2017 National Survey on The First-Year Experience included several that could be conceived as developmental tasks (in order of frequency):

- academic planning or major exploration (a proxy for developing purpose),

- introduction to college-level academic expectations,

- student–faculty interactions, and

- career exploration or preparation (Keup, 2019).

Results from the 2019 National Survey on Sophomore-Year Initiatives found that the most frequently reported campuswide objectives were career exploration or preparation and academic planning (Hartman & Young, 2021). Relative to the first year, the developmental tasks associated with the sophomore year begin to move away from learning norms and expectations and coalesce more strongly around developing purpose. Schaller (2005; 2018) highlights the importance of commitment to purpose for sophomore-year students in their development as they move through developmental periods of random exploration, focused exploration, tentative choices, and commitment.

Another key aspect of the developmental viewpoints used to describe transitions include the role of student-as-identity. In these depictions, students' development is described as the "shift from one identity to another" (Ecclestone et al., 2010), and student identities are characterized by their change of status in or occupation of particular roles. For instance, there are forms of identity that can be described as those contextualized within the role of being a "student," namely major, career, civic engagement, or transfer status (see Musoba et al., 2018; Smith & Gayles, 2017; Zhang et al., 2019). Through the developmental lens, identity shifts consist of more than the mere passage of time or a shift in situation. Instead, transitions represent psychosocial movement from one status or stage to another, such as movement from one's status as a member to their identity as a participant.

The role of time in conceptualizations of transition as development stands in contrast to previously mentioned frames, such as transition as movement or adjustment. In theorizations of adjustment and movement-based transitions, time bounds and defines the transition itself (beginning, middle, and end). In contrast, through a developmental lens, time itself does not "guarantee transition to the next stage" (Gale & Parker, 2014, p. 742; see Coertjens et al., 2017; Little & Mitchell, 2018; Selznick & Mayhew, 2019; Sharma & Yukhymenko-Lescroart, 2018; Shim et al., 2017; Shim & Perez, 2018; Vaccaro et al., 2019). Rather, the focus shifts to leveraging available time to optimize development. This perspective is evident in the concepts of involvement (Astin, 1984) and student engagement (Kuh et al., 2008), which are used widely to describe, study, and understand student transitions as developmental experiences (see An & Taylor, 2019; Johnson & Stage, 2018; Niehaus, 2017; Pérez, 2017; Trolian, 2019; Turk & González Canché, 2019). At the core of these perspectives is: (a) a recognition that time is a fixed and scarce resource and (b) the view that qualitative features of an educational experience will maximize student outcomes (i.e., improved learning and development through transitions) that occur during a specified timeframe.

Naming and Facing the Challenges with Transition as Development

As was the case with movement, adjustment, and stability, certain tensions must be named when transitions are conceptualized as development. Too often, developmental images of transitions are presented as part of a progressive, cumulative, and irreversible process. However, studies show examples of students in transition moving forward and then backward, or backward and then forward as they encounter the developmental tasks associated with their transition experiences. When describing the experiences of students in the second year of university study, Schaller (2018) pointed out that the developmental process is often not as linear as our models present them to be: "Exploring, meandering, drifting, or floundering all have a different feel to them and a different impact on students who are in transition" (p. 25). Also, regression between stages might actually represent progress, and students could experience multiple stages at any given time (Schaller, 2005). Similarly, Jabbar et al. (2021) noted that many students' paths toward transfer were not linear, sequential, or easily bound by time.

Further, when we describe student transitions along "paths," we must be cognizant of who has agency in creating the pathway. Pallas (2003) noted that "pathways are well-travelled sequences of transitions that are shaped by cultural and structural forces" (p. 168). So it goes for transitions as development: institutional responses that set learning and development objectives for students "place significant onus on students regarding their commitment and motivation to study, engagement with learning, interaction with staff, and participation in out-of-class activities" (Gale & Parker, 2014, p. 739). This onus is placed on students because transitions-as-development situates the phenomenon at the student level, relating to their internal world of meaning-making and identity. As such, institutions "construct [students in transition] both as the problem and solution to increasing retention" (Weuffen et al., 2021, p. 121).

Now we can add transitions as development to the table from the previous section, which has been amended in Table 2.2. In addition, we can also add a new element, the temporal dimension, which helps us understand definitions of transition as movement, adjustment, and stability more clearly as well.

Table 2.2.

Key components of conceptualizations of transitions as movement, adjustment and stability, and development

| | Transitions as: | | |
Dimension	Movement	Adjustment and Stability	Development
Main image or metaphor	Movement of students between educational institutions	Critical moment initiates a psychological process of adjustment into, through, and out of a challenge brought about by change	Psychosocial movement from one developmental stable state or stage to the next. Punctuated equilibrium

table continues on page 25

table continued from page 24

Dimension	Transitions as:		
	Movement	**Adjustment and Stability**	**Development**
Institutional role	Creating policies that facilitate, ease, or smooth movement between institutions (e.g., high school to university)	Creating conditions that afford students the supports needed to adjust toward social and psychological stability	Describing desired developmental "outcomes" and creating educational environments that make the best use of time as a scarce resource to maximize student development
Orientation to student	External: Concerns related to transitions are with policies, systems, and processes in which students participate	Internal: Student must contend with psychological challenges brought about by changes in the environment	Internal: Development occurs as students move from one stable psychosocial state to another
Agency	Institution is centered as agentic; transition terms are set by institutional systems, policy, norms	Institution is centered as agentic; critical points in time and environments are institutionally constructed. Students are respondent; they must contend with adjustment and accommodation into institutional setting	Institution is centered as agentic; developmental milestones and stages are preconceived as paths shaped by the institution. Students are respondent; they must navigate the meaning-making and identity formation being directed by institutional objectives
Temporal view	Movement localized and situated in time. Critical junctures predictable at time points such as the first year	Adjustment period situated in time, its beginning marked by a critical event or an unrealized, yet anticipated happening	Periods of growth not easily marked by critical point or passage of time. Irreversible forward movement by students through transitions

Transitions as a Sociocultural Process

Let's take a moment to step back and acknowledge that up to this point, views of transitions have discussed students' movement—whether psychological, emotional, or physical—between environments without examining the environment itself. However, transitions are situated within "social, cultural, and organizational contexts" (McDonough, 1997, p. 9). What role do institutional environments play in transitions? This is largely what models of transitions as a *sociocultural process* are trying to communicate and encourage us to examine.

In sociocultural models of transition, institutions of higher education represent new cultural settings, environments, and surroundings into which students arrive. These perspectives consider how entering and engaging with the social structural features of the new social environment lead to acquisition of knowledge, skills, and dispositions associated with (ongoing) membership in colleges and universities. This is variously described as a process of separation, transition, and integration by Tinto (1975), socialization by Bean and Metzner (1985), Weidman (1989), and Vacchi and Berger (2014), or by the accumulation of forms of cultural and social capital by researchers such as Nora (2004), Laanan et al. (2010), O'Shea (2016), and Richards (2022). While there might appear to be similarities to what we previously described in the section on movement, adjustment, and stability, the difference here is that the process is described as an individual's orientation to the social environment or culture, as opposed to the internal psychological process of adjustment.

Sociocultural perspectives on transitions highlight an "interactionist" perspective, or the importance of the interaction between the student and the environment (Bassett, 2020; McCormick et al., 2013). A major assumption, tenet, and conclusion of these perspectives is that student success—as frequently defined by persistence or retention, both signals of acculturation into the institution—is predicated on (a) the interaction of the student and the institutional environment and (b) the mutuality of the commitment of the student to the institution and the institution to the student (McCormick et al., 2013; Rusbult & Arriaga, 1997; Savage et al., 2019). An important perspective the sociocultural transition framework illustrates is the institution's role in creating supportive cultural conditions for student transitions.

More recently, research, theory, and scholarly practice literature have engaged ecological systems perspectives in describing the interactionist viewpoints on student transitions. The ecological perspective put forth by Bronfenbrenner (1979) has been employed to highlight the ways the interactionist perspective must account for the multiplicity of proximal environmental influences (e.g., peers, faculty, staff, family) as well as those more distal (e.g., institutional policy, curriculum, sociocultural trends) that influence student transitions (see Fish & Syed, 2018; Hallett et al., 2020; Iloh, 2018;

Renn & Arnold, 2003). Kezar and Kitchen (2020) argued that thinking about sociocultural transitions through an ecological systems lens was important because "student experiences in multiple contexts within and beyond college (e.g., classroom, family, living spaces, college events) shape their learning, development, and outcomes and … student development is best understood holistically" (p. 225).

One feature of research and theoretical literature that employs a sociocultural perspective on student transitions is the importance of acculturation of students into both the academic and social worlds of the institution (e.g., Bean & Metzner, 1985; Nunn, 2021; Tinto, 1975; Vacchi & Berger, 2014; Weidman, 1989). Contemporary researchers continue to draw on the Tintonian concepts of *academic* and *social integration* as key drivers of retention, persistence, and graduation, so-called "RPG" objectives, as well as successful transfer (e.g., Andrews, 2018; Baker et al., 2020; Franke & Bicknell, 2019; Goldberg et al., 2019; Hartman, 2023; Johnson & Stage, 2018; Kamer & Ishitani, 2019; Kopp & Shaw, 2016; McCormick et al., 2013; Shirley, 2021; Turk & González Canché, 2019; Wolniak, 2016; Xu et al., 2018). This ongoing attention to academic and social integration is not without its issues, as it forms an expectation of assimilation (Tachine et al., 2017) and, as Bassett (2020) points out, "according to Tinto's theory, the students themselves are primarily responsible for their lack of integration" (p. 355).

In addition, sociocultural conceptualizations of transitions frequently describe how processes of acculturation or socialization are mediated by important individuals who are proximate to students in the cultural ecosystem. These may include those internal to the institution (e.g., faculty, staff, and peers) as well as those external to the institution (e.g., family, employers, and members of students' communities). Berger and Milem (1999) point out that Weidman's model differs from Tinto's in that "students who successfully integrate into the academic and social subsystems of a college do so not at the expense of their home backgrounds, but because of them" (p. 661; see Rucks-Ahidiana & Bork, 2020 for a summary of research supporting this point).

Drawing on social belonging theory, Salusky et al. (2022) suggests college students have a natural human desire to connect with communities that include *relatedness*, emotional connection marked by care and concern, and frequent interaction with others. Thus, transitions are related to the individual's ability to make meaningful connections with others—including those who are knowledgeable about the community and able to validate students' experiences (Hallett et al., 2020; Hughes & Gibbons, 2018; Jenkins et al., 2021; Kezar & Kitchen, 2020)—and the openness of the community to allow for meaningful participation of the individual (Attinasi, 1989; Carter et al., 2013; Lave & Wenger, 1991).

Naming and Facing the Challenges with Transition as a Sociocultural Process

Many critiques have pointed to potential problems with the notion that students should be responsible for their own integration—academic, social, or otherwise—into an institution of higher education. Such criticisms point to the important role communities play in student acculturation (see Attinasi, 1989; Hurtado & Carter, 1997; Koo et al., 2021; Rucks-Ahidiana & Bork, 2020; Tierney, 1992; Tinto, 2012; Yao, 2015). Subsequent critiques of sociocultural approaches to understanding college student retention and transition home in on the notions of separation and integration. Hurtado and Carter (1997) noted that many students did not, in fact, separate from prior communities. Many students attend part time, have serious responsibilities outside their college environments, and represent post-traditional students whose lives do not reflect traditional models commonly used to consider and frame important transition issues (Hurtado & Carter, 1997). As a result, it becomes clear that "a strong 'separation' assumption [is]… not … a necessary condition for transition and incorporation (integration) in college" (Hurtado & Carter, 1997, p. 339). Following Hurtado and Carter's lead, recent research has drawn on subsequent revisions and critiques of Tinto's theory, emphasizing the importance of students' psychological sense of community, a sense of belonging, fit, or getting-in (Attinasi, 1989; Cole et al., 2020; Hurtado & Carter, 1997; Nora, 2004; Nunn, 2021; Schreiner et al., 2020a; Strayhorn, 2012; Yao, 2015), rather than focusing on separation and integration (see Duran et al., 2020; Murdock-Perriera et al., 2019; Oxendine et al., 2020; Pokorny et al., 2017; Rucks-Ahidiana & Bork, 2020; Strayhorn, 2012; Tachine et al., 2017).

When we talk about transitions as a sociocultural process, we must consider the social structures into which students enter, not simply accept them as neutral (Tierney & Venegas, 2009). Vacchi and Berger wrote about the challenges student veterans face during their transitions: "The transition difficulty of joining an academic community and the challenges to student success have to do with the differences in socialization and culture between academia and the military" (Vacchi & Berger, 2014, pp. 105–106). Therefore, the questions that face defining transitions from a sociocultural point of view include: Socialization to what? How does a student become socialized? On whose terms does the socialization happen?

Expanding on the questions of *to what* and *on whose terms*, the sociocultural perspectives on transition expand on some ideas we have previously described while opening paths to others. Far too often, students report that to transition represents an exchange: In order to gain access to important funds of cultural or social capital, students who are members of communities for which higher education was not historically built to serve (to wit: Black, indigenous, Latinx, disabled, LGBTQ+, female, low SES, among many others) must change the terms of their interactions with previous communities. Carter et al. (2013) call out that "it is difficult for minority students in hostile campus racial climates to integrate into the social and academic systems" (p. 103). Moreover, when transitions are viewed through the lens of theories that focus on academic and social "integration," students are positioned to feel that attending college represents a choice between changing themselves to fit in and honoring the communities they desire to remain connected with (see Nora, 2004; Rodriguez & Mallinckrodt, 2021; Wilson et al., 2018), an exchange in which they are literally selling out.

We can now add another column to our table keeping track of components of conceptualizations of transition: transitions as a sociocultural process. This information will be useful as we continue to build to a definition of college student transitions.

Table 2.3.

Key components of conceptualizations of transitions as movement, adjustment and stability, development, and sociocultural process

	Transitions as:			
Dimension	**Movement**	**Adjustment and Stability**	**Development**	**Sociocultural Process**
Main image or metaphor	Movement of students between educational institutions	Critical moment initiates a psychological process of adjustment into, through, and out of a challenge brought about by change	Psychosocial movement from one developmental stable state or stage to the next. Punctuated equilibrium	Interplay between the social structures within the institution and the socialization to that cultural environment as experienced by the student
Institutional role	Creating policies that facilitate, ease, or smooth movement between institutions (e.g., high school to university)	Creating conditions that afford students the supports needed to adjust toward social and psychological stability	Describing desired developmental "outcomes" and creating educational environments that make the best use of time as a scarce resource to maximize student development	Facilitating sociocultural "integration" into the institution's cultural environment; creating climates aimed at supporting students' commitment and psychological sense of belonging

table continues on page 30

table continued from page 29

	Transitions as:			
Dimension	**Movement**	**Adjustment and Stability**	**Development**	**Sociocultural Process**
Orientation to student	External: Concerns related to transitions are with policies, systems, and processes in which students participate	Internal: Student must contend with psychological challenges brought about by changes in the environment	Internal: Development occurs as students move from one stable psychosocial state to another	External/internal: Socialization is represented by an interaction between the student and the institution. Concerns may arise because of movement between cultures and differences in orientation to them.
Agency	Institution is centered as agentic; transition terms are set by institutional systems, policy, norms	Institution is centered as agentic; critical points in time and environments are institutionally constructed. Students are respondent; they must contend with adjustment and accommodation into institutional setting.	Institution is centered as agentic; developmental milestones and stages are preconceived as paths shaped by the institution. Students are respondent; they must navigate the meaning-making and identity formation being directed by institutional objectives.	Institution is centered as agentic; socialization to institutional culture can be viewed as the primary task of the student in transition. Students are respondent or target groups; "successful" transitions predicated on student commitment and internal feelings of fit or belongingness.

table continues on page 31

table continued from page 30

| | Transitions as: | | | |
Dimension	**Movement**	**Adjustment and Stability**	**Development**	**Sociocultural Process**
Temporal view	Movement localized and situated in time. Critical junctures predictable at time points such as first year	Adjustment period situated in time, its beginning marked by a critical event or an unrealized, yet anticipated happening	Periods of growth not easily marked by critical point or passage of time. Irreversible forward movement by students through transitions	Images of socialization, integration, and commitment dependent on time available to students. Time and place matter as students move back and forth between cultural settings.

Transitions as Becoming

The final form of conceptualizations and descriptions of transitions follows what Gale and Parker (2014) described as *transition as becoming*. Transition-as-becoming is not conceived as a response to a particular episode or event; a process of stage-based development; or simply a change in identity or group membership, but "as the experience of changing" or becoming (Gorgorió et al., 2002, p. 24). As such, transitions, and the tensions they represent, are no longer conceived as singular and episodic events; rather they are fluid, ever-present, and everyday features of any learning environment. Thus, the being that is shaped through transitions is "always in process" and "consciously and unconsciously created" as students interact with their college environments (Anzaldúa, 2015, p. 69).

Thus, students do not simply enter college, remain there, and experience learning in an institutional vacuum; rather, they frequently move back and forth and in and out of a variety of spaces (Renn & Arnold, 2003). Transitions-as-becoming are not neatly bound or localized in place and time, instead they include ebbs and flows and movements forward and backward. Schooler (2014) presented a conceptualization of college transitions of Native American students that illustrates this becomingist perspective. Her model describes student transition and growth in a circular pattern where student transitions might not start and end in predictable stages and where the model could expand and shrink, depending on the student's needs and situation. Becoming responds to one of the challenges we pointed out with transitions framed as development: The becomingist perspective holds that transitions are not necessarily linear and recognizes that development occurs in multiple directions (e.g., backward and forward, both on and off campus), which more accurately represents most learners' lived experiences (Bowman et al., 2019; Gale & Parker, 2014; Jabbar et al., 2021; Schaller, 2018; Taylor & Harris-Evans, 2018).

Student experiences of being and becoming can contrast their past and present experiences with an imagined and expected future state, a concept known as *self-continuity* (Fish & Syed, 2018) wherein "their sense of being-in-the-future and being here-and-now [are] interwoven" (Hamshire & Jack, 2016, p. 1910). Thus, transitions as experienced by students are dynamic and represent the interplay of internal (student) and external (institutional) forces (Gale & Parker, 2014; Schaller, 2018). This suggests at least three key implications about the relationship between the institution and student that arise from the perspective of transitions-as-becoming.

First, this perspective acknowledges transitions can be full of anxiety and risk and are often challenging, unsettling, or troublesome experiences. Indeed, that same anxiety and risk, while difficult to negotiate, can be transformative, powerful, and productive, leading to positive change and catalyzing new learning (Bunting & Williams, 2017; Gravett, 2021; Rodriguez & Mallinckrodt, 2021). Resultantly, this perspective rejects the notion that transitions necessarily represent crises or problems that must be solved, removed, or eased by the institution (Gravett, 2021; Quinn, 2010). For example, Hatch et al. (2018) found that the challenges present in a first-year community college student success course (e.g., uncertainty and motivation) interacted with structural and pedagogical elements of the course to create "a low-stakes rehearsal space for developing a college-going identity that transcend[ed] the particular form of the activities" and led to a new college-going literacy (Hatch et al., 2018, p. 140).

Second, transitions-as-becoming must consider the multiplicities present in students' lives, in particular those students from groups historically excluded from full participation in higher education, such as Black, Latinx, indigenous, low-income, and disabled students (Anzaldúa, 2015; Barry, 2005; Fish & Syed, 2018; Gale & Parker, 2014; Rodriguez & Mallinckrodt, 2021; Zerquera et al., 2018). Students' multi-faceted and interwoven identities call for transition theory and practice that is inclusive, relevant, and connected to students' lives (e.g., Barry, 2005; Gale & Parker, 2014; Hurtado et al., 2012; Miles, 2000; Museus et al., 2017). For example, Yosso's (2005) conceptualization of *community cultural wealth* has been employed by researchers in studies on transitions and points to the importance of creating pedagogical spaces that are collaborative, inclusive, and culturally relevant (see Liou et al., 2009; Pérez et al., 2018). This requires institutions to be engaging, open, and accepting of the individual and the assets they bring with them (Gravett, 2021; Yosso, 2005).

Third, transition to college or university represents the mutually constituted relationship between student and institution. As a result, the becomingist perspective again requires us to attend to the role of power in the student–institution relationship. While the institution will naturally be in a position of power, it can make moves to be more open. This openness should include not only allowing the student to be an agent, but also receptiveness on the part of the institution to be changed by the student(s), leading to what we might consider as *co-agentic spaces*. When this occurs, both the student and institution can realize successful outcomes. Openness can lead to a mutual commitment between student and institution, a factor that researchers have connected to transition and successful completion of students' educational programs (Savage et al., 2019). As Attinasi (1989) pointed out, "persistence behavior is a consequence of a process in which the student is an active participant and related to the manner in which the institution becomes and remains, through everyday social interaction, a reality for the student" (p. 251).

Naming and Facing the Challenges with Transitions as Becoming

Presentations of the conceptualization of transitions as becoming also pose challenges. Frequently, descriptions of becoming in transition are (rightly) centered on the student and fail to address relationships with others in academic communities and the roles they play in becoming in transition. These descriptions hint at, but stop short of, describing the kinds of relationships with other members of the community that shape students' membership, identity, and becoming.

This is not of trivial consequence. As we have encountered and engaged with conceptualizations of becoming, we frequently have reflected on our own practices working with students in transition. This has led to conversations centered on questions like: "How do becomingist perspectives shape the kinds of interactions and relationships we ought to be having with our students?"

Continuing to work through our rethinking of student transitions, we have found the becomingist point of view to be compelling and aligned with our understanding and theorizing, as well as our experiences in practice working with college students in transition. However, part of the challenge we have noted with these perspectives is the difficulty translating them to practice. Gale and Parker (2014) offered brief recommendations on structures and pedagogies that would be informed by a becomingist view, yet they acknowledged scant examples of the ideas in practice. Commenting on the need for practical application of transitions as becoming, Baker and Irwin (2019) characterized becomingist viewpoints as useful for differentiation between conceptualizations represented in existing research and practice. However, they found those viewpoints fell short of providing a theoretical pathway to understanding "students' real-time transitions into (and through, out of and sometimes back into) higher education, and what impacts upon, facilitates or constrains these shifts" (Baker & Irwin, 2019, p. 79).

Thus, as we lay out our theoretical/practical case in the chapters that follow, we will present ideas for how this apparent theory-to-practice gap might be bridged. Before that, though, let's include transitions-as-becoming as the final addition to our table of conceptualizations of transitions. Table 2.4 outlines some of the key features of transitions conceptualized as becoming.

Table 2.4.

Key components of conceptualizations of transitions as movement, adjustment and stability, development, sociocultural process, and becoming

	Transitions as:				
Dimension	**Movement**	**Adjustment and Stability**	**Development**	**Sociocultural Process**	**Becoming**
Main image or metaphor	Movement of students between educational institutions	Critical moment initiates a psychological process of adjustment into, through, and out of a challenge brought about by change	Psychosocial movement from one developmental stable state or stage to the next. Punctuated equilibrium	Interplay between the social structures within the institution and the socialization to that cultural environment as experienced by the student	Experience of changing; students making meaning of who they are in each community as they reconcile being in some spaces with becoming in others
Institutional role	Creating policies that facilitate, ease, or smooth movement between institutions (e.g., high school to university)	Creating conditions that afford students the supports needed to adjust toward social and psychological stability	Describing desired developmental "outcomes" and creating educational environments that make the best use of time as a scarce re-source to max-imize student development	Facilitating sociocultural "integration" into the institution's cultural environment; creating climates aimed at supporting students' commitment and psychological sense of belonging	Creating educational spaces that are collaborative, inclusive, and culturally relevant; creating opportunities for students to assume greater ownership in authoring their own realities

table continues on page 35

table continued from page 34

Dimension		Transitions as:			
	Movement	**Adjustment and Stability**	**Development**	**Sociocultural Process**	**Becoming**
Orientation to student	External: Concerns related to transitions are with policies, systems, and processes in which students participate	Internal: Student must contend with psychologica challenges brought about by changes in the environment	Internal: Development occurs as students move from one stable psychosocial state to another	External/internal: Socialization is represented by an interaction between the student and the institution. Concerns may arise because of movement between cultures and differences in orientation to them.	Internal/external: Becoming has personal and social aspects. Dialectic of durable self with community-situated and negotiated identity central to learning and transition. Transitions represent the dynamic interplay between internal and external forces.
Agency	Institution is centered as agentic; transition terms are set by institutional systems, policy, norms	Institution is centered as agentic; critical points in time and environments are institutionally constructed. Students are respondent; they must contend with adjustment and accommodation into institutional setting.	Institution is centered as agentic; developmental milestones and stages are preconceived as paths shaped by the institution. Students are respondent; they must navigate the meaning-making and identity formation being directed by institutional objectives.	Institution is centered as agentic; socialization to institutional culture is viewed as the primary task of student in transition. Students are respondent or target groups; "successful" transitions are predicated on student commitment and internal feelings of fit or belongingness.	Both student and institutional actors are centered as co-agentic; Institution exists and has agency to create pedagogical spaces; students bring being and becoming as assets and work toward greater forms of agency through actively participating in institutional communities.

table continues on page 36

table continued from page 35

		Transitions as:			
		Adjustment		**Sociocultural**	
Dimension	**Movement**	**and Stability**	**Development**	**Process**	**Becoming**
Temporal	Movement localized and situated in time. Critical junctures predictable at time points such as first year.	Adjustment period situated in time, its beginning marked by a critical event or an unrealized, yet anticipated happening	Periods of growth not easily marked by critical point or passage of time. Irreversible forward movement by students through transitions	Images of socialization, integration, and commitment dependent on time available to students. Time and place matter as students move back and forth between cultural settings.	Transitions not neatly bound or localized in place and time. Becoming is not linear; transitions can have ebbs and flows or expansions and contractions. Ongoing, ever-present, situated in everydayness

Discussion: Key Takeaways from Our Review of What We Mean by "Transition"

Now that we have catalogued and critiqued these various descriptions and conceptualizations of "transition," we would like to highlight three topics that serve as signposts for the overall landscape. These are important challenges, issues, and points of departure that emerged throughout the previous descriptions but represent issues that cut across all the categories of transition definitions, models, and theories. They also initiate answers to the theoretical and practical questions of:

- What can and should institutions of higher education do about transitions?
- What should institutions consider as they engage in work around transitions?
- How should institutions position themselves vis-à-vis students as stakeholders?

Definitions and Theories Offering Little Guidance for Policy and Practice

One of the things that brought us to this project was a concern that many of the prevalent models or theories of transition described what transitions meant for students but offered little guidance for higher education practitioners in program design. We concede that the policy responses, where transitions are conceived as moving students and credits between institutions (e.g., dual enrollment programs, transfer pathways), offer ways to improve transition experiences for students. Yet, this practical solution falls short of a *theoretical* rationalization of why such a response might matter. Such a description would convey an explanation of what transition is or means, and why this particular policy response might help.

In the next chapter, we will expand on our thinking about transitions as "becoming." But, even becoming as outlined by Gale and Parker (2014) points to a new way of conceptualizing transitions while falling short of providing useful examples of how it might happen or what higher education practitioners, educators, and policy makers might consider in designing practice, research, and policy. As we have illustrated, this can become a way of masking the idea that the institution sets the terms of the transition. When the onus for the transition is on the student, the institution does not have to change its practices fundamentally—it simply has to create structures to inculcate students into its prescribed ways of being.

On the other hand, we would be remiss not to acknowledge the "student success" movement in higher education in which institutions, state systems, and higher education meta-organizations (i.e., national associations and organizations that form an ecosystem of campus leaders to contend with key issues in U.S. higher education) have recognized and redressed the ways their institutions have been shifting responsibility for success onto students. Notable examples include shifting the consideration from "college ready" students to "student ready" campuses (McNair et al., 2016); reconsidering the role, function, and structure of developmental education (Complete College America, 2012); and identifying the institution's role in creating barriers to success in so-called "gateway courses" (Koch, 2017b), among many others. It is our hope that the work we present in the following chapters will boost these reform efforts for higher education in at least two ways: first, by providing theoretical rationale for many of the reforms that have already been made, and second, by providing theoretical and practical guidance for the reforms and applications being designed and implemented.

Problems with Identities, Equity, and Power

As we scanned the literature to catalogue and critique the landscape of theorizations and studies on transition, a critical mass of studies brought to light the transition experiences of students from a number of social identities represented in higher education, including:

- Latinx (e.g., Cuevas, 2020; Nuñez & Sansone, 2016; Pérez, 2017),

- Indigenous (e.g., Fish & Syed, 2018; Oxendine et al., 2020; Tachine et al., 2017),

- Black or African American (e.g., Griffin & McIntosh, 2015; Means et al., 2016; Shirley, 2021; Zerquera, 2019),

- Gender identity (e.g., Flint et al., 2019; Goldberg et al., 2019; McHenry-Sorber & Swisher, 2020),

- Ability (e.g., Garrison-Wade & Lehmann, 2009; Miller, 2017; Scruggs et al., 2021),

- Neurodiversity (e.g., Clouder et al., 2020; Cox et al., 2017; Cox et al., 2020),

- Veteran status (e.g., Griffin & Gilbert, 2015; Lim et al., 2018; Sansone & Segura, 2020; Stone, 2017; Vacchi & Berger, 2014), and

- First-generation status (e.g., Becker et al., 2017; Harper et al., 2020; Palbusa & Gauvain, 2017).

In these studies, the lens of identity is used to illustrate how the developmental and sociocultural processes of transition are not always straightforward or something that "just happens." Far too often, students are required to adopt identities-as-students that are in line with dominant social groups and to abandon their familiar ways of knowing, doing, and being (Gale & Parker, 2014) associated with their multiple identities.

Similarly, because institutions are in the position of power to set the terms of the transition, we must acknowledge the power dynamics inherent in college student transitions. Transitions are shaped by social locations of the individual and the institution. Enrollment patterns show students from various social groups (which are stratified along cultural definitions and constructions of race, gender, class, and ability, among others) are more likely to enroll in institutions that "match" their location on social hierarchies. Not only are eligible students from working-class backgrounds less likely to enter into degree-granting institutions—themselves part of an educated elite—but they also are more likely to enroll in community colleges and declare majors perceived as less prestigious (Quinn, 2010). Moreover, transitions, even when they are conceptualized as the simple movement from one educational state or experience to another, are not uniformly experienced and as such, present issues of equity. Therefore, whatever definition and theory of transitions we offer must account for and attend to student identity, equity of opportunity, and institutional power.

The Dialectic of Institutional and Student Agency: Finding Co-Agentic Images of Transition

Throughout this chapter we have referred to the institution's power while operating under the assumption that its definition and use is widely and well understood. Without getting into a protracted discussion well beyond the scope of this book, we offer a definition of institutional power that suggests it is the ability to bring about the outcomes the institution desires by getting others to do that which they might not otherwise do (Dahl, 1961; Salancik & Pfeffer, 1977) This suggests power influences the autonomy of the students in transition (Bess & Dee, 2008). In other words, when institutions seek to describe or define the outcomes of students during or as a result of transition, issues of students' autonomy and agency are brought to the forefront.

When we speak of students' agency in transitions, we are referring to their capacity, situated in the educational environment into which they are entering, to act in accordance with their own autonomy. Students' capacity to see themselves in a future that includes success framed in their own terms is also a necessary consideration for agency (Emirbayer & Mische, 1998; Quinn, 2010). Thus, to limit students' present and future capacities for being and doing is to limit their agency

If we run down the various types of conceptualizations we have reviewed in this chapter, we can see how the institution, via educational administrators, policymakers, and advocates, is framing the idea of transition in its own terms (Gale & Parker, 2014; Kitchen et al., 2019; Quinn, 2010) regarding success. When institutions set the parameters for the transition, whether psychosocially, emotionally, socially, or procedurally, the institution is exercising its power in ways in which students must acquiesce their agency to participate. Of course, students might exercise agency and choose to leave the institution. But, this point illustrates the tension between institutional and student agency; when institutional agents and policymakers cast departure unilaterally and unequivocally as "failure" in conversations and practices around transition, student agency is not fully considered in the conceptualization.

Many becomingist commentators would suggest institutions should respond to this tension by becoming engaging, open, and accepting of the individual and their cultural assets (see Gale & Parker, 2014; Gravett, 2021; Quinn, 2010; Yosso, 2005). We agree with this point of view and will argue many points aligned with it throughout the remainder of the book. However, to take this argument to an absurd extreme would cast an image of higher education being so open as to lose all meaning—not to mention that resistance to such an idea from faculty, staff, and the public at large would mean such a place could not exist in the real world.

So while we are not suggesting institutions should give up their structures wholesale, we do need ways of thinking about transitions that acknowledge institutional power and agency, while also attending to student agency during transitions. Therefore, we suggest looking for what we are calling *co-agentic* descriptions and depictions of transition. Co-agentic spaces are places and thoughts of theory and practice in which both students and institutions can manifest agency. We offer that co-agentic descriptions and depictions of transition would account for the following considerations:

- institutional and professional discipline/academic community goals,

- the extent that students have participated and been afforded the access and opportunity to participate in the educational practices of the institution in alignment with their own goals for learning and achievement,

- the extent that students can contribute in authentic and meaningful ways to the institution's educational practices on any number of levels (e.g., in the classroom, student success program evaluation, institution-level decision making), and

- the extent that institutional promises for successful skill development, learning, meaningful progress, and participation and contribution can reasonably be delivered.

Conclusion

By now, we hope to have shed some light on the murky theoretical landscape of what is meant when we talk about "transition" in higher education. Through the overview presented in this chapter, it should be apparent that this singular word can represent a multiplicity of meanings and implications, depending on its use and context. We also hope we have illuminated the contributions and drawbacks of the use of each conceptualization of transitions, whether it be movement, adjustment, development, sociocultural process, or becoming.

In the next chapter, we will introduce theoretical foundations for the reimagined definition of college student transitions presented at the beginning of this chapter. As we describe foundational concepts such as situated learning, legitimate peripheral participation, learning by doing, and becoming, we encourage you to consider how these perspectives respond to, challenge, and expand on the conceptualizations of transition presented in this chapter. Moreover, we encourage you to consider how the perspectives presented in the next two chapters could provide new and more accurate ways to think about what we mean by "transition."

Crucial Considerations

The following questions can help guide your rethinking of transition theory and/or practice:

- What do you think of when you envision student "transition"? How is your working theory reflective of one or more perspectives on transition we have presented in this chapter, namely movement, adjustment, development, sociocultural process, or becoming?

- How have you operationalized transitions in research, practice, or policy that you have been responsible for? How has this operationalization shaped the way you consider the student–institution relationship during transition?

- In what ways have you seen transitions conceptualized in research, theory, or practice that have honored the social identities and communities of students? How does this illustrate issues of power and agency at play during the transition?

PART 2:

OUTLINING A NEW THEORETICAL POINT OF VIEW ON TRANSITIONS

Chapter 3 | Laying Theoretical Foundations: Transitions-as-Becoming and Situated Learning

In Chapter 2, we started by offering a new perspective on how we are currently thinking about transitions—or more accurately, thinking about how students experience transition-ing. We contend that student transition represents becoming a member of an academic community through ongoing practice that includes:

- strengthening meaningful connections with others in the community;

- ongoing authentic participation in the practices of the community, leading to increased awareness of and experience with knowledge, skills, tools, and language that facilitate further participation; and

- opening up a trajectory of ways of being, doing, and thinking that are congruent with student goals and images of self.

It bears restating this perspective again here, as in this chapter we will begin to lay the foundations of our reconceptualization of transitions. In Chapter 1, we shared that our rethinking would take the form of *bricolage*, weaving together perspectives taken from research, theory, and practice on college transitions. And so our work as theoretical bricoleurs begins in earnest, with our aim to pull together perspectives that will support the (re)conceptualized vision of student transition(ing) we have shared.

To start, we will spend some time situating our theoretical base in the perspectives of becoming. Next, we will expand on what becomingist viewpoints mean for transitions in college, connecting these viewpoints to transitions-as-becoming presented in Chapter 2. From there, the bricolage will begin to take shape as we introduce *situated learning* and *legitimate peripheral participation* as a way to operationalize and position becoming in practical, policy, and research-based approaches to understanding transitions.

Situating Our Theory in Becoming

Right out of the gate, it is important that we call back to the typology of transitions presented in Chapter 2 and make it clear we are situating our perspective squarely in the transitions-as-becoming camp. Thinking about student transitions as becoming goes back to at least 2010 (and possibly earlier), when Quinn wrote about first-generation working-class students from under-resourced areas in the United Kingdom who withdrew from university before completing their credentials. She described these students' transition experiences as fragmented and complex, punctuated by "forward and backward motions of life and the closures and openings of opportunities to learn" (p. 122). Moreover, she described the change that comes with transition as a "perpetual process" where the "self is constantly reworked" (p. 123).

In their typology of transitions, Gale and Parker (2014) drew on the work of Deleuze and Guattari (1987) to connect transitions with the idea of becoming. At the risk of oversimplification, but in the interest of clarity and connection, we will focus on a few key points from Deleuze and Guattari's (1987) concepts of becoming. The first is the concept of the rhizome. Rhizomes are features of plants that, different from roots, spread in multiple directions at once, connecting many stems and plants that can be seen above ground (some examples of plants with rhizomes include ferns or clonal aspen). The rhizome was appealing as a metaphor for Deleuze and Guattari's (1987) understanding of humans' being in the world because it is non-linear, acentered, non-hierarchical, and ever-connected (Gravett, 2021; Taylor & Harris-Evans, 2018).

Second, becoming is an ongoing process that always has been and always will be in people's lives. Continuing the metaphor of the rhizome, Deleuze and Guattari (1987) note: "A line of becoming has neither beginning nor end, departure nor arrival, origin nor destination. ... A line of becoming has only a middle" (p. 293). This suggests that student experiences of change are fluid, evolving, and subjective (Gravett, 2021), proposing that conceptualizations of transition should consider how "higher education [is] part of the whole life of the student, which notices and views the granularity of students' lived experience" (Taylor & Harris-Evans, 2018, p. 1256). Thus, knowledge, salience, and meaning are situated in time and place—and in individuals. Stability is fleeting. New meanings come from relationships between things in individuals' environment. No two students are the same, because difference is everywhere.

Finally, because becoming centers on the uniqueness of each individual's subjectivity in change and transition, attention should be brought to the manifold ways students experience any community they encounter, including higher education, as part of their life course and the meaning they assign to it. Gale and Parker (2014) assert that "if education systems, structures, institutions and procedures do not take account of the multiplicities of student lives that enter HE [higher education], then transition practices will be less effective" (p. 745). Again, at the risk of oversimplification, this calls to mind the subjectivities of each student in terms of individual identity and the generalized subjectivity that coalesce into social identities. Our theory and practice must account for the realities of both individual and social identities and the ways they influence students' transition-ings.

We find these perspectives to be particularly insightful and useful in opening and widening our understanding of student transitions. In the next section, we will further explore the implications of taking on becomingist perspectives as we aim to further understand and explicate student transitions. We also will continue to build on the perspectives outlined in the description of transitions-as-becoming in Chapter 2.

Expanding on Transitions as Becoming

To bring clarity to and expand upon the ideas of transition as becoming, we offer the following two perspectives situated in becomingist ideas. The first expands on the ideas of how becoming informs descriptions of the ways students experience transitioning. The second discusses how transitions, viewed through a becomingist lens, influence students' sense of self—an important connection to the perspectives on situated learning presented later in this chapter.

Becoming and Experiencing Transition

The idea of becoming opens understanding into the nature of transition for students. As students transition through higher education, they are frequently engaged in processes of redefining the self and assuming greater ownership in authoring their own realities (Baxter Magolda, 2009, 2014; Parks, 2000). College transitions not only facilitate this redefinition of self, but for many students "the transition *require[s]* a redefinition of self and values" (Terenzini et al., 1994, p. 68). Becoming is often how students describe their own successful transitions. They develop pride in the "real learning" they have achieved; namely, learning about oneself, discovering abilities, developing pride in one's competence, and becoming more self-reliant, described elsewhere as exploring a new *provisional self* (Ibarra & Petriglieri, 2010).

Too frequently, higher education professionals describe college transitions as movement into, through, and out of higher education, as though students are trapped and locked in heart, body, mind, and soul for the totality of a degree program. Following this ideal, students enter our campus communities on Day 1 and only leave when family and friends come to collect them at commencement. The truth is, students move into, through, and out of college every single day, and likely multiple times throughout their day. This is true of students of all types, including traditional-age students living a residential college life. They might move into higher education for their 9:30 a.m. chemistry lecture (and if they could have scheduled it later in the day, they likely would have), through it as they chatted with friends and study group members on the way to their next class, and then out of it by noon as they go to work for their afternoon shift at the local grocery store. Later, they move back in as they meet up with other members of their study group, through it as they review the notes from the chemistry class in preparation for their lab the next day, and then out again once the pizza (purchased via a gift card someone got for participating in a clinical trial earlier that week) arrives and their attention turns to a particularly heated episode of an elimination-based pre-marital reality TV franchise. And then, into, through, and out again as they get back to their room in the residence hall to write the paper on 19th century nihilism that is due ahead of their 10 a.m. Tuesday-Thursday class. "So, transition rather than being a rare event is actually an everyday feature" (Quinn, 2010, p. 124).

Thus, transition-as-becoming is not conceived as a response to a particular episode or event; a process of stage-based development; or simply a change in identity or group membership, but "as the experience of changing" or becoming (Gorgorió et al., 2002, p. 24). As such, transitions, and the tensions they represent, are no longer conceived as singular and episodic events; rather, they are fluid, ever-present, and everyday features of any learning environment. As Gloria Anzaldúa (2015) put it: "Identity, as consciously and unconsciously created, is always in process—self interacting with different communities and worlds" (p. 69).

To illustrate the flux that is ever-present throughout a student's time in college, we will turn to a contemporary transitional issue: the sophomore experience. In a workshop on sophomore student success in the fall of 2022, Molly Schaller presented her research on sophomores regarding their academic commitment, development of purpose, and engagement in campus-focused relationships. Schaller pointed out that traditional sophomore-year students might move back and forth on continua of exploration and commitment in each of these arenas of their lives as they engage in self-discovery. Moreover, she shared that although regression might appear to be moving against the developmental currents, it might well be a positive sign for the overall process of commitment. For instance, a student might have worked hard to successfully complete their lower-division course requirements with the aim of moving toward the upper-division coursework in their major. However, the student might realize through this process that their career goals have developed and will require a shift in major to achieve them. This paradox was typified by a metaphor shared by a student Schaller had interviewed; the student said the sophomore year for her was like "thinking you have all your ducks in a row and turning around and realizing they are geese" (McQueen-Ruark & Schaller, 2022, slide 24). Present progress and success are context-dependent, and past successes can transform into signals that point to the need for redefining future markers of success.

Becoming and Students' Sense of Self

New students enroll with hopes that college will change them in meaningful ways. They might hope for increased human capital (e.g., improved skills and greater know-how), expanded social networks, or membership in and affiliation with the institution. And while higher education can deliver on these promises, acquisition of knowledge and skill "are not the most crucial or lasting components of the college experience. Higher education, at its best, changes the lives of graduates" (Hanson, 2014, p. 1). Similarly, "the student who graduates will not be, and should not be, the same person as the one who started college" (Hersh & Keeling, 2011, p. 6). Thus, as students enter new academic communities and (hopefully) begin participating in meaningful ways, they take on new identities, develop novel ways of engaging with the world, and assume fresh ways of being.

Yet, this change does not happen when orientation ends or immediately upon conferral of a degree. It is an ongoing, everyday process that extends beyond learning about or engaging with new rules, tools, skills, and processes. The process has "person-forming properties" (Barnett, 2009, p. 435) and is therefore "about the making of [their] selves, in a process of *becoming*" (Fairclough, 1992, p. 91, emphasis added). When individuals join a college community, they take on the mantle of "student." When those students enter new communities and begin participating in them, they take on new roles, memberships, and identities. They will encounter a multiplicity of new ways of seeing themselves: as an aspiring journalist, as a participant in a management training program, as a member of a Greek-letter organization, as a PSYC 101 student, as a working mother enrolling at the local technical college to take a math course as a prerequisite for a teacher credentialing program, or myriad other identities associated with the new affiliation.

The thing about identity, however, is it is both mercurial and durable. It is something that is situational, negotiable, and portable. It is socially constructed as well as deeply internal and personal (Anzaldúa, 2015; Hanson, 2014). The focus on identity as an aspect of transition leads us to consider transitions that include, but are more than, the immediacy of moving in, moving through, and moving out of any given change the student encounters. Therefore, as Gale & Parker (2014) assert, when thinking about college transitions, we should be less concerned about "isolated and stilted movements from one context or identity to another" (p. 745) and more attentive to the contribution to the student's overall sense of self. This signals some of the key concerns of a *becomingist* point of view, as expressed by Taylor and Harris-Evans (2018):

> *[B]ecoming … describes the immanent unfolding of the 'self'. Becoming is about change as ongoing flux and dynamic flow, as emergence and unfolding in micro-moments and instants. Becoming is the endless play of difference and it is difference that effectuates becoming. Becoming is the working of self-differentiation. It is not change 'within' an entity. Neither is it a change 'from' something 'to' something else. (p. 1262)*

Students' sense of self is fluid and changing and has personal and social aspects (Barnett, 2009; Gale & Parker, 2014; Hamshire & Jack, 2016; Smith, 2009). Students move in and out, back and forth between communities, each with its own culture, makeup, and orientation to higher education (and sometimes these orientations are in conflict with one another). As a result, students are consistently moving back and forth between social positions and must make personal meaning of who they are in each situation, reconciling their different ways of *being* in some spaces with who they are *becoming* in others. Thus, becoming "must be understood as a series of flows, energies, movements and capacities, a series of fragments or segments capable of being linked together in ways other than those that congeal it into an identity" (Grosz, 1994, pp. 197–198).

Drawing on what we presented in Chapter 2 combined with what we have just discussed, we offer the following to summarize key elements of the transitions-as-becoming point of view:

1. Transition is not static. Rather, it is an ongoing and ever-present process situated in everydayness of students' lived experience.

2. Transitions are multi-locational and situated in (various) communities; individuals move in and out of multiple communities and assume varied positionalities as they do so.

3. As transition deals with the ever-present experience of change and the dynamic interaction between student and environment, it suggests active engagement of the learner with the structured learning environment.

4. Transition to college or university represents the mutually constituted relationship between students and the institution. As a result, this perspective requires us to attend to the role of power in the relationship between student and institution.

So, how to continue to build out to our vision of college student transitions that attends to becoming and also offers practical guidance for higher education professionals of all types?

That requires us to go back to the beginning of our thinking about all of this, starting with a fateful conversation over dinner at the ACPA annual convention.

Situated Learning and Legitimate Peripheral Participation

Back in March 2017, we were both members of the ACPA Directorate Board for the Commission on Admissions, Orientation, and First-Year Experience—a subdivision of a large student affairs professional organization, ACPA, with a focus on supporting higher education practitioners who work with students in transition. We had gone out to dinner with members of the board during the annual convention in Columbus, Ohio.

Prior to the dinner, Dallin was working on his discussant remarks for a research paper session the next day on the benefits of student–faculty interaction. He wanted to tie three papers together conceptually, and he was looking for a theoretical explanation for why student–faculty interaction was shown to be an important predictor or condition for college student success. So while we were at dinner, Dallin asked Bryce, "What theories do you know of that help explain why interactions with faculty members matter?"

The benefit of Bryce's voracious appetite for reading, combined with his background in educational psychology, led to a serendipitous moment: Bryce had simultaneously been reading about how learning as *legitimate peripheral participation* (LPP) had potential application for improving how we think about supporting student success. In the ensuing conversation, the two of us speculated that the consistent and repetitive finding that student–faculty interactions led to a host of beneficial outcomes for students could be explained by some of the key ideas outlined by Jean Lave and Etienne Wenger's (1991) description of *situated learning*. In other words, that the magic happens when students and faculty engage in activities that move beyond simply acquiring and transmitting bits of knowledge, toward becoming co-participants in the core learning activities of higher education.

Eventually, we thought about how Lave and Wenger's work could be applied to college student transitions. We had many conversations about how their descriptions of situated learning, participation, and communities of practice illustrated an interesting point of view on how student transitions happen, what higher education professionals could do to support those transitions, and even why some students struggle during transitions. Moreover, as we started getting serious about these connections, we read and found that we were not the first to make the connection between situated learning and higher education transitions (e.g., O'Donnell & Tobbell, 2007; Orsmond et al., 2013; Turner & Tobbell, 2018).

We will use that realization as a starting point for our description of situated learning and legitimate peripheral participation and how, when combined with the concept of becoming, a useful new framework is created for understanding students in transition.

Situating Our Learning of LPP

Not long after the initial conversation, we decided to use conference presentations to share our thinking and get feedback from others who work in supporting student success. For us, a fruitful entry point into this conversation has been asking those in attendance to reflect on a transition they have experienced themselves. We typically ask them to think about how they became a member of their new community, what sorts of opportunities they had to engage with more established community members, what barriers or challenges they faced, and what the key factors were in making their transition successful.

Many of those who generously shared their stories of transition discussed events such as moving into a new area and joining a community organization. Some told us about coworkers or members of a church group who had been around a while taking the newcomers under their wing and showing them the ropes or just making them feel welcome. Some shared about joining new friend groups and feeling like they knew they were starting to belong when they were let in on the inside jokes, and when they felt like they were being seen and accepted for themselves. Others talked about the importance of having some real responsibility, even though it might seem insignificant, but knowing others were counting on them.

These responses contrasted with those who shared times when they felt like their transition stalled because they did not truly feel like members of the community, or that there was a lack of appreciation for who they were. One colleague shared that their transition at a new job was forestalled because, although work leadership said new suggestions and ideas for how they could get their work done were welcome, when the colleague did share opinions or offer novel proposals, they were ignored or not given serious consideration.

As you will see, these responses are not only indicative of the features of situated learning and legitimate peripheral participation (LPP) as outlined by Lave and Wenger (1991), they also signal an approach to think about how and why becoming happens. Indeed, these responses parallel students' transitions into new communities they encounter when arriving at colleges or universities.

Now, we invite you to take a moment and reflect on a transition you have experienced (you will need to humor us and set your book down). What were some of the elements of your transition?

Illustrating Situated Learning and LPP: Apprenticeships of Vai and Gola Tailors

In their original articulation of situated learning and LPP, Lave and Wenger (1991) provided five examples from cultural and historical traditions to highlight the key features of LPP as a process of learning. In this section we will (re)present one of those examples: the training and preparation of novice tailors in the Vai and Gola tribes of Liberia, which, while not rooted in higher education, is useful in seeing how LPP facilitates transition, learning, and becoming.

Apprentice Vai and Gola tailors work in shops supervised by master tailors (i.e., master participants or master learners), who actively engage in both the daily practice of tailoring clothes and the training of apprentice tailors. In fact, the work of training apprentices is situated within the activities associated with tailoring garments in at least three ways:

- Being a tailor and supporting the learning of new tailors are one and the same.

- The apprentices move in and join the household of the master tailor, which situates the learning in an "unfamiliar culture of production" (Lave & Wenger, 1991, p. 70).

- The work of these master tailors is highly visible and public, which is key to facilitating the learning of new apprentices.

Apprenticeships last about five years and involve systematic and sustained opportunities to participate in the actual work of the shop by observing master tailors, as well as *participating* with other apprentices in important, yet novice-level tasks (e.g., making simple hats or children's clothing). Note that these opportunities for observation and participation are structured such that apprentice tailors see the full process of tailoring garments from start to finish. Over time, as apprentice tailors master simple garments, they move on from *peripheral* forms of participation and contribution to more challenging articles of clothing, ending with higher-end formal suits. Again, while new tailors' work is peripheral and rather simple, it is critical to the overall success of the shop and is therefore *legitimate*. New tailors do not work on "throw-away" or "practice" garments. Instead, they are producing actual merchandise to be purchased by real customers. By participating in the actual practices of the shop, they come to know the methods of tailoring and develop the necessary skills to participate in their community of practice (Lave & Wenger, 1991).

Models such as the tailoring apprenticeship provide an interesting foil to more common definitions of learning that describe it as a process of acquiring or accumulating knowledge and skill (Sfard, 1998). In contrast to the *acquisition metaphor* for learning, LPP is grounded in what Sfard (1998) describes as the *participation metaphor*, which characterizes learning as the process of becoming a member of a new community through engaging with more skilled community members in that group's practices and discourse. Learning, then, is situated in both practice and relationships. The mastery of knowledge and skill is a natural outcome of learning and is subsumed in the process of participating in the legitimate activities of the community. Further, learning represents a movement by the learner from a position as a consumer or acquirer of knowledge on the periphery, to a producer and participator in an increasingly empowered position in the academic community.

Applying Situated Learning to College Transitions

Our application of situated learning and LPP to college student transitions starts with a simple premise: College students enter institutions of higher education as novices to an academic community of practice. Now, it is important that the term "novice" not be interpreted to imply that students enter colleges and universities devoid of any knowledge, perspectives, or experiences that will help them navigate the novel environment they find themselves in. What this does imply is that no matter how much students bring with them, when they enter institutions of higher education, they do so just like anyone enters a new community of practice: on the *periphery*. The periphery represents an abstract position in a community that signals the individual has been granted entrance or access but remains near the boundaries or edges of the community; members at the periphery of a community have limited access, exposure, and engagement with the activities within. Peripherality may represent a *limited* position for newcomers, but it is, by its nature, not *limiting*. Therefore, a distinction arises between being in the periphery—as a space that holds the promise of expanding access, roles, participation, and commitment—and being contained in the margins. We explore this distinction further in Chapter 4.

That novice students enter college via the periphery is a fairly straightforward proposition. The question higher education professionals frequently face is "What to do once we have the new student in peripheral spaces on campus?" Based on the illustrative example of the Vai and Gola tailors, and through the perspective of LPP, peripherality implies that it should not be conceptualized or crafted as a holding space where students learn about the process of college before they go and do it. Rather, peripherality should provide students with opportunities to contribute in meaningful and authentic ways to the activities of the community; in other words, to learn about college by doing the things that matter to success in college. This progressive *participation* in authentic practices of the community is achieved as students interact, work, converse, and in many cases, live with more experienced members of the institution.

For example, first-year students might live on campus and participate in an engineering living–learning community. Here, they interact with both resident assistants (who were members of the community before assuming their new roles) and upper-division student teaching assistants in their first-year seminar taught by a tenured professor of electrical engineering. This kind of participation is not limited to traditional and residential students. Another example could include a student veteran who comes to campus and, after engaging with the veterans' success center, is invited to fill a peer leadership role to mentor other student veterans while working alongside staff, designing and providing services.

Participation is not limited to engagement outside the classroom, however. As an in-classroom opportunity, a well-crafted biology course invites students to work alongside faculty or more experienced students to engage in the kinds of scientific inquiry a biologist would use to answer questions about the differences between plants with roots and those with rhizomes.

Lave and Wenger refer to participation in tasks and responsibilities that are authentic and meaningful to the community as *legitimate* forms of participation. Moreover, these legitimate forms provide (relative) newcomers with opportunities to get involved with the practices of the academy in increasingly skillful and intentional ways, leading to increasing competence and familiarity with the knowledge, activities, and discourse of the community.

It is important to note that terms such as *legitimate* have been used to justify the exclusion, oppression, and marginalization of people, primarily those who have been minoritized in many ways including race, ethnicity, gender, sexuality, religion, social class, and disability. We have limited the use of the term legitimate to this discussion, and throughout the rest of the book we have used terms such as authentic, genuine, and meaningful, among others, to point to this notion. It is true that retaining the use of these terms is also not without challenges related to power and agency. Rather than shying away from the complex power relations that LPP suggests (Lave & Wenger, 1991; O'Donnell & Tobbell, 2007), we find this feature of LPP useful to account for the role and use of power and agency. We'll dive more deeply into that throughout the rest of the book, with a particular focus in Chapter 5.

As such, Lave & Wenger's (1991) description of situated learning is insightful as applied to college student transitions, including the processes by which they become experienced students capable of both academic and social success in their new environments. One important lesson from this application is that transitions and meaningful learning are inseparable and are characterized by the degree that new students are enabled to participate with more experienced students, faculty, and staff in the intellectual life of the institution, not simply by acquiring new knowledge or skill. Thinking about transitions as becoming through increasing forms of participation does not minimize the need for foundational knowledge or skill among new students. Instead, it demands higher education professionals shift our focus from procedure, knowledge, and skill acquisition as the primary outcomes of efforts to support student transitions to a focus that provides students in transition with opportunities to engage with others in the practices that both require and develop foundational knowledge and skill.

Consequently, the quality of new students' learning and transitions depends heavily on a range of environmental factors, including access to opportunities for engagement in authentic academic practices; proximity to and meaningful involvement with more experienced learners; and an underlying institutional culture that recognizes all new students as being capable of participating in and contributing to the academic community (Nunn, 2021; O'Donnell & Tobbell, 2007; Sfard, 1998). Moreover, "learning cannot be separated from the context in which it takes place" (Caffarella & Merriam, 1999, p. 63). This is how transition and learning are situated in the institution and the full lives of students in transition. "In contrast with learning as internalization, learning as increasing participation in communities of practice concerns the whole person acting in the world" (Lave & Wenger, 1991, p. 49).

It is important here to recognize that Lave and Wenger set out to describe how learning can happen in informal ways, and they were clear to make distinctions between LPP and formal instruction (Lave & Wenger, 1991). Notwithstanding, we contend that through a becomingist lens, transition is a form of situated learning as Lave and Wenger described it. Situated learning involves participation in an activity system with more experienced members in a community of practice. Therefore, transition, if it concerns membership in any given community of practice in an educational environment, cannot occur without some degree of learning as Lave and Wenger defined it. While transition is learning, it is situated learning. Think of it like a classic SAT response: All transitions are learning, but all learning is not transition.

In sum, college transitions require (a) meaningful engagement; (b) with faculty and peers; in (c) authentic activities; that (d) introduce new students to the knowledge, skills, tools, and mindsets that, over time, move them toward increasingly complex and advanced participation in the campus community.

The Bricolage: Becoming and Situated Learning

This chapter has provided a description of transitions as becoming and an argument for the application of situated learning and legitimate peripheral participation as a way to think about students' transition to higher education. The question now is, "How do becoming and situated learning come together to provide a description and conceptualization of college student transitions that attend to becoming and relationships, while also offering practical guidance for higher education professionals?"

Becoming

Situated learning opens understanding into the process of becoming for students by describing how becoming, participation, and learning are all part of the experience by which we engage with and make meaning in and of the world during transitions. Learning and identity formation are not separate processes, but "are interactive and shape each other as they evolve" (Keeling, 2004, p. 10). As Wenger (1998) illustrated, "[learning], in its deepest sense ... concerns the opening of identities—exploring new ways of being that lie beyond our current state. ... It places students on an outbound trajectory toward a broad field of possible identities. [Learning] is not merely formative—it is transformative" (p. 263).

As students engage and participate in the communities of practice they encounter upon arrival and throughout their experience in higher education, they also engage in the development and ongoing (re)negotiation of self and being. Students find themselves taking on membership and new roles in academic, professional, and extracurricular spaces. Moreover, becoming can either give students the space to deepen their own identity development along lines of race, class, gender, sexuality, and ability, or it can create marginalizing structures that widen bicultural chasms and force students to choose between being in some spaces, becoming in other spaces, and ceasing to be or become as others (Kaufman, 2014). Therefore, if becoming is situated in everydayness and this is how students form meaning, identity, and connection with the environment and the community, then the question we must confront and intentionally return to is: "How are we as higher education professionals creating the everyday conditions that facilitate participation and contribution in which becoming is situated?"

Relationships

This question points to the important role relationships play in becoming—and situated learning gives us some guidance toward understanding the forms, terms, and purposes of the relationships that are needed during transitions. As students enter and encounter new educational environments, engaging with peers, staff, and faculty is central to learning how to be and do in the academic community. This happens as students do what members of the community do; therefore, it is essential that students, staff, faculty, and administrators interact, engage, and become co-participants in the authentic practices central to the community's functioning.

Relationships envisioned as co-participation in authentic practices of the community are fundamental to creating communities that support a sense of purpose and belonging (Hamshire & Jack, 2016). Participation with others is pivotal in forming a sense of belonging, as it is an essential feature of developing an identity as a member of the community. But simply taking up the identity of being a student is insufficient to engender belonging. Students must take on and internalize the notion that they are situated in the community of their institution, not just as abstracted students who do not belong to an institutional home. As such, membership and purpose situated in a community of practice are key to students becoming learners and creating internalized commitments to studying, engaging, participating, and success.

Moreover, the interdependence that comes when novice students engage with (relative) old-timers in the authentic practices of the campus helps students develop a more internalized source of authority. "Interdependent learning and problem solving in which educators share authority with learners guide learners in refining their internal voices to construct their beliefs, values, identities, and social relations" (Baxter Magolda, 2014, p. 31). This interdependence is key to the becoming that is essential to the transitions students will face during their educational experiences in college and in the other facets of their lives.

Practical Guidance

One of the most exciting applications of situated learning to the notion of transition as becoming is that together, we can start to picture what kinds of practical guidance such a theory can offer. We will spend more time on recommendations for application and practice through the chapters to come, but we can start with some of the guiding principles for practical guidance the bricolage can offer.

If becoming is contingent on, or even connected to, progressive forms of fuller participation, we have to acknowledge that fuller participation is not inevitable and some activities may be well intentioned but will ultimately result in maintaining students on the periphery (O'Donnell & Tobbell, 2007). This requires us to reexamine the underlying assumptions within many of the common transition programs that have a long and storied history in higher education, including first-year seminars, orientation, transfer programs, and senior capstones, among others. When reconsidering these time-honored transition support programs, we must consider the notion that becoming comes through the everydayness of participation. Thus, our focus must turn to the whole of the student experience and not just what we teach or how we teach it (O'Donnell & Tobbell, 2007). Finally, whatever practical guidance we offer must accurately match the lived experiences of students who are experiencing transitions. We cannot just say we are supporting transition without a clear understanding of what it means, how it happens, and what our roles are in it.

Conclusion

Our goal in this chapter was to lay the theoretical foundations for a rethinking of student transitions by bringing together perspectives related to transitions as becoming and situated learning and legitimate peripheral participation. This theoretical bricolage helps us understand the kinds of activity systems that students encounter and are expected to manage when they enter institutions of higher education. Moreover, it provides a theoretical rationale for our definition of student transitions wherein students become members of an academic community through an ongoing process that includes:

- strengthening meaningful connections with others in the community;

- ongoing authentic participation in the practices of the community, leading to increased awareness of and experience with knowledge, skills, tools, and language that facilitates further participation; and

- opening up a trajectory of ways of being, doing, and thinking that are congruent with student goals and images of self.

Moreover, we see transitions as a progressing dynamic activity system, in which students are agentic actors who have meaningful connections with other agentic actors, who have formal and more experienced roles in a collection of communities that comprise an institution.

In the next chapter, we will build on this definition of transitions by offering further explanation of three interrelated perspectives on transition: community, participation, and becoming. These three modes of transition will demonstrate how the blending and application of becoming and situated learning present the basis for a vision for the theory–practice of transition that can set up higher education professionals to improve research, policy, and practice.

Crucial Considerations

The following questions can help guide your rethinking of transition theory and/or practice:

- Thinking about the ways Deleuze and Guattari describe "becoming" in terms of non-linear, subjective, and ever-present features of people's lives, how have you seen such features in the lives of students in transition?

- How might understanding student transitions as being composed of "the experience of changing" shape the way you think about transitions in your research, theory, or practice? What are the implications when we consider the ways transitions are context dependent and that markers of success might not be static for students or institutions during their time in college?

- What examples of situated learning or legitimate peripheral participation in transition have you seen? What are the potential communities of practice into which students are granted access? What opportunities for authentic participation toward becoming full participants of the community of practice are offered?

- How might participation in the authentic practices of any given academic community of practice alongside more experienced members of the community open up lines of becoming for students in transition?

Chapter 4 | Framing the Theory: Community, Participation, and Becoming in Transitions

So far, we have described why we need improved thinking on how transitions are conceptualized and operationalized in research, policy, and practice; offered a revised definition of transitions; and outlined the theoretical basis for new thinking about transitions. At this point you are likely wondering, "How does this all come together?"

One cold December day in Utah, we spent the morning asking ourselves this question, and three main concepts kept rising to the forefront: community, participation, and becoming. We ultimately created a concept map outlining the key ideas connected to each of the three, and this became foundational to our subsequent thinking, presenting, and writing on transition theory.

But what to call these three concepts? Were they features, aspects, or perspectives? No, they do more than simply describe what a transition is. Were they tenets, principles, or properties? In some ways, these descriptors fit, as community, participation, and becoming comprise what happens during successful and transformative transitions, but those labels seemed to imply an idea that was divisible into discrete elements. Pathways? Perhaps, but that applies more to community and participation than becoming. They certainly were not stages. So, what were they?

Modes of Transition

As we prepared to share these ideas at the Annual Conference on The First-Year Experience in February 2022, we had to decide what to call them. After trying a few of the previous labels, we considered "mode." This idea first made sense based on a common understanding of the word as the way or manner something is expressed or done, such as a mode of transportation (Oxford English Dictionary) or getting into *work mode* (Merriam-Webster). But this idea became even more appealing when we realized mode can also refer to a form, arrangement of being, or manifestation of an underlying substance (Merriam-Webster; Oxford English Dictionary). This description seemed to fit our view of the role of community, participation, and becoming in transitions. But that's not all.

Community, participation, and becoming are not only integral parts of the transition for the student and the institution, but they are also *how the transition itself happens;* they are the modi operandi of transitions. Yet, each one as modus—or mode—is inseparable from the others. In short, as students *participate* in *communities,* they *become.* It is important to acknowledge that these modes are always present and that transitions always happen, regardless of what educators do or what transition-focused initiatives exist. Therefore, the questions of "What community?" "What kind of participation?" and "What kind of becoming?" become central to concerns of transitions and their respective modes.

Theory often operates as a metaphor, providing a particular framework or lens that magnifies specific features of a phenomenon. However, as certain features are illuminated, others are obscured. Thus, while a focus on each mode highlights important features of college transitions, concentrating on only one leaves the overall picture incomplete. Although we can describe key features of each mode that support transformative and socially responsible college transitions, we must attend to the fact that a dynamic interplay exists between community, participation, and becoming. They do not occur in isolation as discrete elements and, while it is possible to account for each of them separately from an initial design perspective, they must be considered as a unified whole in practice.

Notwithstanding, in the sections that follow, we describe each of the three modes: *community, participation,* and *becoming.* A deeper exploration of the connections and interplay between them will come in the next chapters.

Community

Transitions are inherently about change. But the trouble with change is that it nearly always leaves us feeling unmoored and disconnected. We believe much of the discomfort students experience comes from what Parker Palmer has described as the *pain of disconnection* (1993). Accordingly, transition work in higher education is, at least in part, about helping students reconnect—with peers, faculty, academic interests, and communities that offer safety and support. These positive aspects of membership in a community are critical because "learning is always a perilous undertaking" (Parrish, 2009, p. 516).

Recent research in student affairs has emphasized the importance of helping students experience a *sense of belonging* (e.g., Duran et al., 2020; Means & Pyne, 2017; Murdock-Perriera et al., 2019; Nunn, 2021; Oxendine et al., 2020; Pokorny et al., 2017; Rucks-Ahidiana & Bork; 2020; Silver, 2020; Strayhorn, 2012; Tachine et al., 2017), which strongly contributes to overall emotional and psychological health. Likewise, a sense of belonging fosters the confidence necessary for students to engage more fully with the transformative elements of their transition experience (e.g., new relationships, new ways of thinking, new challenges). Ultimately, the type of learning we associate with (successful) transitions is aimed at enabling students to more fully become participants with both their peers and their professors in the social and intellectual lives of their institution. More simply put, transition happens as students come to belong and hold real membership in a patchwork of communities that, together, help them feel a sense of belonging on campus.

Our hope is that the thinking we share in what follows will help to expand readers' conception of community. This includes a wider variety of the forms or manifestations that might "count" as community, as we work together with colleagues on our campuses to design spaces that offer varied forms of community belonging to students from a diverse range of backgrounds and identities.

What Do We Mean by Community? Why Does It Matter for Transitions?

So, what do we mean by community? Of course, community includes a network of social relationships that help a student feel safe, comfortable, and supported among a group of peers with whom they share common interests or goals. However, a sense of belonging in a social community is just one of a variety of ways that students can experience the benefits of community during times of transition. We hope this book helps readers broaden their view of community beyond simplistic notions of social ties with peers (Smith, 2018). We find Lisa Nunn's recent work on college belonging valuable in this regard. It gives a nuanced perspective on three distinct forms of community students might experience during college: (a) social community, defined as a feeling of friendship and acceptance among small peer groups; (b) academic community, characterized by confidence in the classroom and academically based relationships; and (c) a feeling that one belongs to the wider campus community (Nunn, 2021).

From this perspective, community is layered across multiple aspects of the student experience rather than being viewed as a monolithic and generalized "campus community" to which a student belongs. For example, a student might have one community of friends they see on weekends; another community with members of a campus club; a learning community of peers that study together for their math class; and a more formal academic community in the chemistry lab where they participate in undergraduate research. So, on the role of community in transitions, what we really are advocating for is attention to helping students establish a constellation of inter-related communities. Much like a safety net with a multitude of interwoven ropes, such constellations provide holistic support and stability across the various domains of students' transition experience.

What Does the Research Reveal about the Characteristics of Communities That Support Transitions?

While students can and should experience belonging across a variety of communities, research on student success and college transitions points to key characteristics of communities that contribute to successful transitions and position students for transformative growth. We have chosen to focus on three aspects of effective communities that can help inform the way we offer support to students in transition: (a) a troubling of the dichotomy of "social" and "academic" communities; (b) relationships with more experienced members of the community; and (c) opportunities for participation, contribution, and ownership.

Troubling The Dichotomy of 'Social' and 'Academic' Communities

In our attempts to build community, practitioners sometimes are guilty of failing to recognize the need to facilitate connections and relationships that are both social *and* academic in nature. As a number of researchers have made clear, successful college transitions are influenced by various domains of the student experience including academic performance, social relationships, and emotional well-being (e.g., Braxton et al., 2004; Kuh et al., 2007; Tinto, 1993).

However, following more recent research and depictions of student transitions (e.g., Duran et al., 2020; Hurtado et al., 2012; Rodriguez & Mallinckrodt, 2021; Schreiner, 2010, 2020; Strayhorn, 2018), we contend that the dichotomy between social and academic communities might be more interwoven for students than many prior models depicted. For example, Schreiner's (2010, 2020) construct of *thriving* has broadened the field's conceptualization of student success and highlighted the need for a more holistic view of success that incorporates academic success, interpersonal relationships, and psychological well-being. Seen through this lens of thriving, when students are part of communities that bring together both their academic and social experiences, they find a greater overall psychological sense of community, which research has connected to higher levels of academic success and persistence toward educational goals. In such communities, social relationships with peers grow out of shared academic interests and collaborative academic projects.

High-impact practices such as undergraduate research, learning communities, internships, and study abroad programs are excellent examples of experiences that facilitate communities in which the notions of "academic" and "social" start to blend. While such experiences include a significant intellectual component, they also bring students into academically focused relationships based on common learning goals. Such experiences have tremendous potential for supporting students in transition: They allow students to align their identities as participating members of academic communities, as well as strengthen their sense of belonging as they find congruity among the social connections they make.

Relationship-Rich Experiences with More Experienced Members of the Campus Community

Students' relationships with faculty and staff are equally important. Indeed, research from the past three decades suggests that meaningful interactions with faculty members might be some of students' most impactful experiences (e.g., Chambliss & Takacs, 2014; Kim & Sax, 2017; Mayhew et al., 2016; Tinto, 1993). Similarly, when academic advisors are part of a student's academic community, they can help connect students with resources, invite reflection on the learning and growth experienced during transition, and both scaffold and broker experiences that connect students with additional communities of practice, launching them toward expanded opportunities for future participation (Felten et al., 2016; Schreiner, 2018). Institutions can facilitate these connections by providing students with access to learning communities, seminar courses, and residential living settings that involve faculty and academic advisors in intentional ways and foster frequent interactions between students and staff.

In addition, relationships with peers in the community are important and powerful (Astin, 1993; Mayhew et al., 2016; Shook & Keup, 2012). In fact, in their comprehensive synthesis of research on how college affects students, Mayhew et al. reported "overall peer interactions ... probably have the second largest impact of any form of interpersonal experience" (p. 553) and have a bearing on such things as academic self-concept, autonomy, general learning, and retention and graduation (Mayhew et al., 2016; Shook & Keup, 2012). As students interact with their peers, in particular those who have greater amounts of experience on campus, they learn what it means to be members of the various communities present on a campus. This is an important role that peer leaders or peer educators (e.g., tutors, resident assistants, orientation leaders, supplemental instruction leaders) play as they provide advice, support, and knowledge (Collier, 2015). Moreover, this role has benefits for the peer leaders themselves. When students become peer leaders, they are engaging in more advanced practices of the community. As a result, they learn while helping mentor their peers as they "model the successful college student role" (Collier, 2015, p. 15).

Participation, Contribution, and Ownership

In addition to providing students with important social capital, effective communities offer students experiential learning that extends beyond mere involvement, to real *contribution* to the work of the community. The literature on thriving describes this as *ownership* (Schreiner, 2018) or *influence* (Nelson et al., 2020) and emphasizes the importance of giving students in transition access to communities where they can actively participate in decision-making processes, lead out in planning and implementing programming, or contribute to the work of the institution in other visible ways (e.g., peer leadership, meaningful campus work study, student government).

Moreover, participation, contribution, and ownership are not only possible in large-scale involvement requiring time outside of class. When students participate in classroom discussions that contribute meaningfully to the learning environment, they demonstrate ownership on the scale of the classroom. Granted, this does not happen automatically; the instructor has to create and lean into the vulnerability in this space for this kind of community to develop and flourish.

In one of Dallin's recent first-year seminars, contribution and ownership were made as explicit expectations of students in the course through a conversation on "How do we engage in a group discussion?" In this conversation, students showed trepidation. Some did not feel they had expertise to contribute, others shared not knowing what awkward pauses meant, and some wondered what the professor was thinking, both during their contributions as well as in times of silence. Yet, after the conversation about what group discussions were like and what role students had in making them successful, the students gradually took increasing ownership in that space and contributed based on their interpretation of the material as well as their experiences.

All these sorts of community involvement, whether large or small scale, not only deepen students' knowledge and skill but serve as *educative* experiences (Dewey, 1938). They open the door for students to progress toward more advanced forms of participation with more expert communities, both on and off campus (Lave & Wenger, 1991).

What Are the Implications of This Focus on Community? How Can It Help Support Transitions?

At this point, it seems helpful to step back and briefly discuss why we feel so optimistic about the focus on the mode of community as such an important aspect of supporting students in transition. Thus far we have largely focused on practical concerns related to prioritizing community in transitions. Now we shift our attention to some of the ethical considerations related to community and transitions: (a) delivering on the promise of higher education and striving for institutional integrity; (b) acknowledging the role of power and privilege in college transitions; and (c) shifting the onus of responsibility for finding community from students to institutions.

Institutional Integrity: Delivering on Our Promises

One of higher education's claims is that it prepares students to be more engaged, informed, and skilled members of future communities, whether that is a disciplinary community or the broader national or global community. However, too often we are guilty of "involving [students] in the community of [higher education] in some ways while keeping them at arm's length in others" (O'Donnell & Tobbell, 2007, pp. 317–318). Or, similarly, we operate under the assumption that we have provided access to community simply by admitting students to campus (Palmer et al., 2009). This subtle denial of access and relegation to the margins of the institution cuts students off from some of the most important elements of a liberal education, namely the opportunity to fully participate in the fundamentally democratic work of collaboratively applying academic knowledge and expertise to address meaningful challenges and vexing questions. An attention to community anchored in involvement with diverse communities and real-world challenges makes good on higher education's promise to prepare students for full participation in civic and economic life upon graduation (AAC&U, 2020).

Power and Privilege in College Transitions

In drawing attention to the need to offer community to students in transition, we also offer a caution: Do not fall into the trap of embracing the perspective that students need to abandon previous identities or communities to become fully integrated into their new communities on your campus (Hurtado & Carter, 1997; Tierney, 1992; Tinto, 1975; Yosso, 2005). This perspective is particularly pernicious for students whose identities align with groups who historically have been excluded from higher education because it imposes steep ethical costs on those striving for upward mobility (Morton, 2019).

We argue, instead, for a reconceptualization of what it means to join new communities—one that views participating in higher education as an additive process that does not necessitate breaking ties with family and friends, surrendering membership in prior communities, or losing one's own sense of identity. In fact, when students are allowed to enter their new community spaces as their authentic selves—complete with their prior experiences, values, memberships, and identities—not only are they more likely to experience thriving in transition, but the existing campus communities they join are revitalized, renewed, and strengthened by the addition of their diverse backgrounds and perspectives (Lave & Wenger, 1991; Nunn, 2021; Rodriguez & Mallinckrodt, 2021; Schreiner, 2020; Tachine et al., 2017). This does not just happen, however. Institutions and the individuals who comprise them must first become aware of their own histories, traditions, and privileged forms of knowing and then must seek to understand, acknowledge, and support the funds of knowledge that students bring with them.

Shifting the Responsibility for Finding Community from Students to Institutions

If we are to provide equitable pathways to transitions, we must do more than just tell students to "get involved" or "find your place." Instead, we need to embrace a more sociologically oriented view of community grounded in the acceptance that the onus for creating and offering community lies with institutions (Durkheim, 1897). For students who have historically been held in the margins (i.e., first-generation students, students of color, low-income students), the invitation to "get involved" or "put yourself out there" is only helpful insomuch as there are communities willing to offer or extend belonging to them (Nunn, 2021). A simple example: Many institutions encourage students to become involved in undergraduate research with faculty mentors. This is a noble and research-backed aim. However, it is one thing to tell students to "get out there" and find a research opportunity. It is much more meaningful for a campus to prioritize equitable access to this high-impact opportunity by proactively identifying students with minoritized identities and connecting them with faculty who can provide entrée into a new academic community.

Participation

The notion of participation as a critical aspect of transitions is not necessarily new. The lexicon of higher education is full of concepts that invoke participation, including *involvement* (Astin, 1984), *engagement* (Kuh et al., 2008), and *quality of effort* (Pace, 1982). However, our review of the literature on transitions suggests a theoretical murkiness around what researchers and practitioners mean when they refer to the concepts of involvement, engagement, or participation. Consequently, we assert that the principle of participation has come to operate as a sort of *cryptotheory* (Yanchar & Gabbitas, 2011)—a hidden or unarticulated cognitive framework that fails to adequately describe the key characteristics of experiences that support transitions. After all, no student experience is absent student participation or involvement—all students participate in the educational enterprise in some form or another. The key issue that should concern us as researchers and practitioners is the nature and quality of student participation (Dewey, 1938).

Why Does Clarifying Understanding of Participation Matter for Transitions?

A lack of conceptual clarity about the role of participation in transitions threatens precision of research and analysis, limits further theoretical development, and ultimately leads to misalignment between stated objectives and the design and delivery of transition programs (O'Donnell et al., 2016; O'Donnell & Tobbell, 2007; Palmer et al., 2009). Again, current discourse around the role of involvement and engagement in the student experience belies the extent that we have thoughtfully considered how to leverage the mode of participation to support high-quality student transitions. Indeed, our inability to speak coherently about what we mean when we claim that "students need to be offered opportunities to participate" or "students need the chance to be involved" suggests a need for new theory and language to guide our efforts to develop transition policy, transition practice, and transition pedagogy.

Building on perspectives from Lave and Wenger (1991), we assert that successful transitions are marked by students' movement from peripheral or novice levels of participation to fuller forms of participation in which they are prompted to actively contribute to the core activities of academia. For example, traditional approaches to orienting new students have largely consisted of attempts to *induct* (Gale & Parker, 2014) students as new members of the campus community by ensuring their familiarity with relevant policies, resources, and tools. When orientation is grounded in a paradigm where transition is viewed as induction, a new student's role is to be a consumer or acquirer of new knowledge or skills. Likewise, the institution takes on a paternalistic role as omniscient provider or dispenser of the discrete bits of knowledge and skill needed for college success.

Viewing participation in this more nuanced way (i.e. participation as contribution) helps students move beyond being passive recipients of information during their transition. This movement from consumer to contributor honors students' abilities to "not only contribute individually to the community as a whole, but ... to influence the community for its good" (Nelson et al., 2020, p. 70). Moreover, a focus on student contribution opens opportunities for ways of knowing, doing, and being that have historically been held out of higher education, thus creating a more open, accepting, and inclusive environment (Gale & Parker, 2014). The notion of contribution sets participation apart from previous conceptualizations of involvement or engagement (Astin, 1984; Kuh et al., 2008). Contributing through participation implies the engagement or involvement is focused, purposeful, in relation with others, and builds up both the community and the participating individual.

In the next section, we outline the key features of participation that help to move the work of supporting transitions beyond induction toward providing opportunities for students to not just "fit in" on their new campus, but to join with their professors and peers in the core academic activities of the academy (e.g., uncovering new ways of knowing, critiquing, and analyzing ideas; engaging in critical dialogue with other learners). While we acknowledge the important transitions work that has taken place over the past decade, we simultaneously respond to calls for refinement, clarification, and broadening of theorizing around transitions (Gale & Parker, 2014; O'Donnell et al., 2016; O'Donnell & Tobbell, 2007; Worth, 2009).

What Types of Participation Support Transitions?

Again, our identification of participation as an essential mode of transition is not a claim that some campuses support transitions by denying students of all opportunities to participate. Instead, our goal is to help readers understand what the best forms of participation look like in practice by describing three key characteristics that define what we mean by participation: authenticity, peripherality, and continuity.

Authenticity

We find much alignment between our thinking and Sanders' (2018) assertion that the ultimate objective of college is to support students in *becoming learners*. Further, with Caffarella and Merriam, we hold that "learning cannot be separated from the context in which it takes place" (1999, p. 63). We emphasize the importance of *authentic* practices. Such practices do not simply serve the purposes of a "transition program"—no matter how well liked or well intended—and then have no meaning outside that program. Consequently, the forms of participation offered to students in transition must, as much as possible, include opportunities to engage in the same practices as more experienced members of the institution—practices that matter to the campus community.

Care must be taken to scaffold this participation to the appropriate experiential level of learners, of course, but even the newest college students can be invited to engage in the learning and becoming process in authentic ways. These could include being invited to debate significant political or social issues using empirical data or established theoretical frameworks in a gateway course; writing for a real audience by authoring an op-ed for the campus newspaper as part of a writing course; or participating in undergraduate research as part of the first-year experience (e.g., Seifert et al., 2019).

Empowering Peripherality

Rather than marginalizing newcomers, peripherality should provide access to people, conversations, resources, and experiences that position novices for progressively advanced forms of participation, more sophisticated ways of knowing, and more complex skill. Thus, peripherality simultaneously refers to a position within a community as well as a potentiality. All potential members of any community will enter into the community via the periphery. Movement toward greater participation is not an inevitable prospect for students, however. Peripherality necessarily connotes the potential for greater participation and contribution. As we stated in Chapter 1, denying students access to the people, practices, conversations, and resources essential to helping them become fully participating members of their campus community is *marginalization*. To hold students in positions of marginality creates communities with a core and an outer ring of people who have been granted token access, which is where transitions too often go wrong for students from groups historically underserved by higher education.

Productive and empowering peripherality positions students to both form relationships with and participate alongside others in their learning community. As described previously, this access to community membership—via participation in authentic practices with others in the community—is critical to supporting transitions. We find it important to echo previous researchers who point out that participation is not inevitable; while peripherality might be granted, access to contribute to the community's meaningful activities may not (Brown & Duguid, 1991; O'Donnell & Tobbell, 2007). Additionally, this type of peripherality aligns with Sanford's (1967) timeless call to provide students in transition with both challenge and support by offering opportunities for engagement and contribution that deepen student learning, but in ways that are within students' developmental reach (see Vygotsky's [1978] conceptualization of the *zone of proximal development* for an in-depth discussion of this idea).

Continuity

The most powerful forms of participation not only facilitate in-the-moment learning but also catalyze future learning by opening the door to richer, fuller, and more sophisticated forms of experience in the future. Put another way, the programs, interventions, coursework, or resources institutions provide to support students in transition should expand students' opportunities for future participation.

A practice common on nearly every campus is the idea of the sequencing of coursework. Students who complete an introductory accounting class should be able to expand their knowledge of accounting practice by enrolling in the next course in the sequence. Similarly, the kind of learning and doing that happens in initiatives that comprise a first-year experience (e.g., orientation, first-year seminars, common reading experience, first-year advising) should directly set students up for possible participation in the authentic practices of college.

Programming designed with this objective for student transitions meets the criteria for educative experience outlined by Dewey (1938) in his foundational work on experiential education. Further, a focus on continuity is a key aspect of approaching transitions as a process of becoming, which we will discuss in greater depth later in this chapter. We return to the notion put forward by Wenger (1998): Participation opens trajectories of doing and being that expand our current states and abilities. It creates possibilities that did not previously exist and presents "shifts and developments in identity and agency" that are part of the process of becoming somebody (Ecclestone et al., 2010, p. 7).

What Are the Implications of This Type of Participation? Why Does It Matter?

So, what does this all mean, especially for folks whose day-to-day, boots-on-the-ground work is focused on supporting transitions?

First, there is a silver lining that gives us great hope for higher education's ability to offer meaningful forms of participation for students in transition: high-impact practices (HIPs). For well over a decade, higher education leaders have known that certain experiences such as service learning, capstone courses, first-year seminars, study abroad, and internships provide powerful educational benefits to students and hold promise for closing equity gaps. However, institutions have unnecessarily delayed participation in most HIPs (save maybe first-year seminars and common reading experiences) until the second half of the student experience. For students fortunate enough to persist to that point, these HIPs are a powerful way of helping them navigate transitions into careers and graduate school. But what would happen if campuses looked to infuse participation in these experiences earlier in the student experience? This would, no doubt, require careful analysis and allocation of resources and require a high degree of collaboration among campus stakeholders. Yet, we are intrigued by the potential results.

Second, the type of participation we describe here is likely to require a shift from what we term a *technical* response to supporting transitions, consisting of large-scale, one-size-fits-all programming focused on induction, to a more human and personalized response. The aim is to prioritize (a) proliferation of a variety of participatory opportunities for students to select from and (b) personal support and mentoring from academic advisors, faculty members, and peer educators who can help students identify which forms of participation will benefit their individual situation most.

Finally, just as we have suggested in our discussion of the mode of community, careful attention must be given to dynamics of power and privilege when considering the role of participation in transitions. O'Donnell and Tobbell (2007) wisely remind us that: "When peripherality is a position from which an individual can move forward toward fuller participation, it is an empowered position. When peripherality is a position from which an individual is prevented from fuller participation, it is disempowering" (p. 326).

Thus, for institutions embracing the approach we argue for in this book, it will be critical to regularly step back to evaluate how students are experiencing peripherality and participation, particularly those who historically have been excluded from engagement in HIPs. If racially and ethnically minoritized students, or those from low-income backgrounds, are consistently being held in disempowering marginalization, transition experiences become miseducative and narrow opportunities for future growth. Our responsibility as educators is to intentionally design environments and experiences that promote social mobility and reject supremacy and oppression in their many forms (e.g., those built on hierarchies based on race, gender, sexual orientation, ability, and religion, to name a few), as well as academic caste systems that uphold systemic inequities.

Becoming

Becoming is central to our conceptualization of transitions; it is both process and outcome, journey and destination, means and end of student transition. As soon as a student arrives at new forms of being, those forms serve as points of departure; therefore, outcomes, destinations, and ends become exploratory vistas from whence new paths emerge. However, as these arrivals happen in historical and cultural contexts and through students' everyday activities, transition is no longer a unidimensional process of movement, adjustment, or development, rather it is "an entangled, nonlinear, iterative and recursive process, in which students travel in irregular ways through the various landscapes of their experience (university, family, work, social life) and bring those landscapes into relation with each other" (Taylor & Harris-Evans, 2018, p. 1256).

As we elaborate and expand on becoming as a mode of transitions, we hope the new—and at times complex—concept of becoming starts to become clearer. Moreover, we hope it serves as a richer way to understand how students are experiencing transitions and how institutions can organize their efforts to support student becoming.

How Are We Thinking about Becoming as a Mode of Transition?

In Chapter 3, we presented an in-depth overview of transitions as becoming. In lieu of rehashing what was articulated there, what follows is an expansion of the concept of becoming and its role as a mode of transition. To illustrate its role as a mode, we will discuss two concerns related to becoming that emerge during student transitions: (a) membership and identity and (b) personal transformation.

Membership and Identity

Earlier in this chapter, we explored the notions of community and belonging. Part of becoming is established when students enter communities in higher education and can start feeling and developing belongingness. The internal, psychological sense of community students develop depends on their feeling like they are members of that community (Nelson et al., 2020). Consequently, the converse is also true: When students feel a sense of belongingness in their campus communities, they are able to adopt the identity as a member of that community. Communities can foster the identity as a member of the group by communicating messages such as those outlined by Nelson et al. (2020): "You belong here and your presence is needed; You have a voice here and you can change this community for the better; Your needs are met here and you can be proud of this community; and You can connect here and meaningful relationships are available" (pp. 71-72).

In this way, transition is not simply learning about being a student. Being a community member who is valued and able to contribute to the community's ongoing formation is central to the transition. Applying Brown and Duguid's (1991) take on workplace learning to college transitions: "[L]earning is best understood, then, in terms of the communities being formed or joined and personal identities being changed. The central issue in learning is *becoming* a practitioner not learning *about* practice" (p. 48). Thus, becoming in transitions is concerned with becoming and engaging with new identities such as student, (insert college team nickname here), pharmacist, learner.

As students engage in participatory and contributory ways in their campus communities, they not only take on new ways of seeing themselves and being, they learn and grow. Thus, "learning, development, and identity formation can no longer be considered as separate from each other, but … are interactive and shape each other as they evolve" (Keeling, 2004, p. 10). This is no more important than in the academic disciplines that students will encounter. When students pursue membership and develop identities in disciplinary communities, they start to be able to think as social workers, talk like economists, and tell stories about their becoming nurses. And so, they are more capable of describing "what they were like before they started and who they became during the course of their education" (Hanson, 2014, p. 8).

Personal Transformation Across Place and Time

If we are not careful, the preceding conversation might come across as a description of transition as development, with identity development the core concern of transition. However, the personal transformation that takes place for students is not usually as straightforward as membership as a binary (e.g., non-student or student, undeclared or emerging chemist, student at the University of Alaska or student at Pima Community College), or identity as a progressive and linear trajectory.

The first things that becoming as a mode of transition troubles with developmental perspectives on membership and identity are the notions of place. As we referenced earlier, students move somewhat sporadically through the various landscapes of their lives, and college is only one of those. We might even suggest the transgressive notion that college does not even crack the top five most important aspects of life for many students! But even when college is among the most important settings in their lives, the multiple communities interact and shape how the student is becoming in each of them. For instance, the academic self-concept of first-generation students has been shown to be shaped by messages from familial groups, such as parents' positive or negative messages about the student's ability to succeed in college (Covarrubias et al., 2020). Thus, the transition cannot be decontextualized from the situation in which the student encounters it, nor can it be disconnected from the situation the student's identity, growth, and capacity are actively creating (Sfard, 1998).

In addition to these concerns with place shaping student being, time plays an important role in understanding the personal transformation that happens within and shapes transitions. As we shared in Chapter 3, transition is a perpetual process situated in the everydayness of students' experiences. Students form and reform their identities as they move back and forth between their communities, affiliated or not with the colleges or universities they are enrolled in.

The grounded theory model of transition for Native American college students described by Rodriguez and Mallinckrodt (2021) clearly exemplifies this process. For Native American students in this study, decisions made before attending college actively affected ongoing anxiety and concerns around the transition and acculturation to college. Moreover, the researchers' description of transition showed that time and place were interconnected. The students discussed how their transitions formed connections to new places while also deepening connections to their previous communities and native cultures. In doing so, they showed that students' understanding of self and being is not only about who they are in their current location but also connects with remembrances and current and future visions of self in other locations, especially those with greater salience—places one might consider "home." This result also evokes images of the future: As the Native American students developed a stronger internal resilience, their transition naturally continued beyond their time in college. Therefore, the students' personal transformation in the transition they experienced was expansive across time, place, and identity (Rodriguez & Mallinckrodt, 2021).

What Are the Implications of Becoming? Why Does It Matter?

Now that we have outlined what is meant by becoming as a mode of transition, the question remains: Why does any of this matter? We offer four answers with an eye toward addressing theoretical, empirical, and practical concerns:

- movement beyond simplistic notions of induction and development,

- meaning and purpose for educative challenges,

- increased likelihood for transformative and high-impact experiences during transitions, and

- implications for defining and measuring "success" in college student transitions.

Beyond Simplistic Notions of Induction and Development

An understanding of transitions as becoming provides a broader view of how students might experience transition. Too often, transitions are reduced to helping students understand their new environments or new identities. In contrast, the *becomingist* perspective invites educators, policymakers, and researchers to understand how transitions are situated in students' lives across multiple communities, between identities, and across the college timespan. One example of this move toward a becomingist theory of transitions is Sanders' argument that college is best conceptualized as the process of *becoming a learner* and that those students who experience this type of becoming are best positioned for future success upon graduation (2018). Here, we would point out that if learning is an ongoing process of becoming, then becoming a learner does not suggest there is a final, stable psychosocial state designated for "learners." Instead, this process acknowledges the ongoing and ever-present identity shifts college students experience. Indeed, when students experience learning and becoming in transition, they carry those experiences beyond higher education as they prepare for the transitions they will encounter throughout their lives (Ecclestone et al., 2010; Gale & Parker, 2014; Sanders, 2018).

Providing Meaning and Purpose for Educative Challenges

When students enter and move toward fuller participation in new communities, they are faced with the real possibility of loss or failure, particularly as they navigate ethical decisions about how to enter their new college community while maintaining ties to past communities and previous identities (Morton, 2019). Students can find transitions difficult, troubling, and unproductive (Ecclestone et al., 2010). We, as educators, should work to reduce systematic, cultural, and procedural challenges and barriers to transition.

Transitions need not be seen as crises, however. When students encounter risks, trials, or challenges, they face a choice to either shield themselves from difficulty—potentially inhibiting growth—or to fully embrace these challenges and work toward an integration of their various community memberships and identities. Choosing to embrace the productive unfamiliarity of transitions provides opportunities for transformation and becoming that moves beyond induction and respects individual differences.

Transformative Experiences in Transitions

When students take on difficulty, challenge, and risk—even when they might appear to fail—and then make meaning of these experiences, they are engaged in a process of becoming. Again, this does not mean we should ignore real barriers to access and authentic participation or place artificial and oppressive difficulties in students' paths for the purpose of somehow "building character." But, as Barnett (2009) points out, we exist in a world characterized by "supercomplexity" (p. 439) and the reality that the knowledge and skills acquired in college are quickly outdated and likely insufficient to respond to novel and unpredictable situations that will appear after students graduate. Baxter Magolda (2014) refers to these as "adaptive challenges" and states that college students must experience the kinds of transformative learning that require increasingly complex ways of making meaning and "capacity to determine their beliefs, identities, and social relations" (p. 26). In other words, transitions rooted in becoming not only set students up for success in college but also prepare them for the unseen vicissitudes of life that await them after graduation.

Implications for Defining and Measuring "Success" in Transitions

The previous implications point to a concern for higher education professionals who work to support students in transition. The question that arises is: "Who gets to determine what success looks like?" Previously we pointed to scholars who have observed that the terms of the transition are usually set by faculty, student affairs staff, administrators, and policy makers (Kitchen et al., 2019; Quinn, 2010). This frequently reduces the complexity of transition and becoming to practical, procedural, and developmental outcomes that primarily meet the needs of those who hold institutional power. We accept the argument that the institution has a stake in defining learning and development objectives and assessing student progress toward those objectives. Further, a focus on metrics of movement, adjustment, and development can provide useful insights that lead to higher rates of success.

However, we suggest that understanding transition as becoming could improve the assessment and evaluation of student learning and development in important ways by considering how "success" is defined on the student's terms. Take the real-life example of a high-achieving student who enrolled at a large, prestigious university in their home state for several reasons, including: the institution's overall academic profile, the campus life and opportunities for involvement, and a successful football team the student has followed since childhood. In addition, the student held the internalized belief that to attend other public institutions in the state would be perceived as not meeting their potential, a phenomenon researchers and policy analysts commonly refer to as "undermatching." Yet, this student had a clear vision of the career they wanted to pursue, and the university did not have a major with a direct path to this professional field. So, the student started taking classes toward an available major and faced a challenging gateway course that they ended up dropping just before the add/drop deadline. As early as the first semester, the student began considering transferring to a different university in the state that had the exact program that would lead directly to the career they were interested in pursuing. The question of "Who gets to determine what success looks like?" again takes stage.

From the institutional point of view, if this student stops out after the first or second semester and later enrolls at another university, this is counted against persistence, retention, and graduation metrics and is therefore operationalized as a failure. Yet, for this student, from the point of view of becoming, the successes are manifold. First, the student had to engage in self-reflection and metacognition to determine whether committing to the institution or their career path was more important. Second, they had to consider what the emotional and financial costs would be to stick it out in a major that was not a good fit for them or the career path they wanted to pursue. Finally, the student was faced with the challenge of determining whether the external formulas and sources of authority they relied on previously would serve or fail them in this scenario, leading to developing the building blocks for an internalized voice of authority (Baxter Magolda, 2014).

Understanding transitions as becoming requires thinking more deeply and completely about how we define and think about what makes a transition "successful." From the student's perspective of completing their education on their terms, all of the achieved results count as successes. The question here goes back to co-agency; in other words, what does success look like for both students and the institution? More importantly, what meaning do we as institutional actors make when we receive certain signals about student transitions? We speak more directly about assessment of student transitions in Chapter 5.

Conclusion

At this point, it should not be hard to see how the modes of community, participation, and becoming are related, particularly because the description of each was not possible without calling attention to features and principles occurring in descriptions of the other modes. We offer final thoughts about how community, participation, and becoming can offer broader insight into student transitions and move us toward the more practical concerns that our discussion of transitions to this point suggests.

First, it is important to acknowledge that attention to community, participation, and becoming is already happening on many campuses and is represented in scholarly practice and research literature. Across these sites are examples of spaces where students find community, meaningfully participate and contribute, and learn, grow, and become the people they want to be. However, we contend that just because many examples of the application, consideration, (re)presentation, and implementation of these ideas exist, educators should not eschew the importance of thinking about transitions and the three modes discussed in this chapter. We believe conceptual and theoretical clarity about how transitions happen, how students experience them, and what matters while they occur will provide a framework for how to understand and intentionally respond.

Second, as an example of how this framework helps us do this, we point to the conversation about the ways that troubling the dichotomy between social and academic communities is an important aspect of understanding student experiences in transition. This idea suggests interested higher education professionals should look for ways to create spaces where social and academic communities can be more intentionally integrated across functional and divisional lines. Keeling et al. (2007) pointed out that student transitions was one of the issues in higher education that cut horizontally across institutional silos. This suggests the framework of the three modes of transition could serve as a natural provocation for cross-functional conversation, leading to collaboration. If working groups already exist, this theory could be used to breathe new life into the conversation.

That brings us to our third point: Because transitions are ongoing concerns of becoming, they take time. The ongoing history of the study of students in transition and the current movement toward improved student success illustrate at least an implicit understanding of this point. The spread of attention from the first year to the sophomore year, to the senior year, to transfers, developmental education, gateway courses and so on, shows the field is aware that transition is an ongoing and multifaceted process. Thus, we must acknowledge that whatever we do to deepen our understanding of or support for community, participation, and becoming will take time. Naturally, this could privilege students who have a greater ability to spend time and find pathways to high-impact practices that offer greater opportunities for participation and relationships across campus. Because of this possibility, we must find ways to identify, create, and resource pathways for those students who might not come by these practices naturally.

In addition, transitions' ongoing nature does not mean that meaningful transitions cannot happen for part-time students or students who cannot engage in co-curricular activities, for whatever reason. It does suggest that we must meet those students where they are and investigate and provide opportunities for them to meaningfully participate in authentic practices of the community, so they can benefit from the promises of higher education.

Finally, you will note that this theoretical discussion of the integrated nature of these modes could not happen without calling on practical examples for evaluating and improving approaches to supporting college students experiencing transitions. Now we can start considering the questions of: How do we do this? And how can we build these perspectives into our practices on campus? In the chapter that follows, we contend with the theory–practice translation that will both deepen the discussion of community, participation, and becoming and begin to illustrate the dynamic interplay across these three modes of transition.

Crucial Considerations

The following questions can help guide or initiate conversations with key partners on your campus or in your research networks and serve as starting points for rethinking transition theory:

- When you think about the importance of community in transitions, what stands out to you? How can institutions of higher education help students develop meaningful relationships and ownership across their academic and social communities?

- What kinds of participation have you witnessed as an important part of student transitions in college? In what ways can institutions create possibilities for ongoing and authentic forms of participation that will help students move from peripheral to fuller participants in the academic and social communities of college?

- How have you observed or experienced the becoming that happens during transitions? How can institutions more accurately evaluate and make sense of the becoming that happens as students encounter educative challenges during transformative and high-impact experiences? How can definitions of "success" be more reflective of the becoming on both institutional and student terms?

- What are ways you have seen the interplay between the three modes of transitions: community, participation, and becoming, as we have described them here?

PART 3:

CONNECTIONS, APPLICATIONS, IMPLICATIONS, AND EXPANSIONS

Chapter 5 | Theory and Practice

The work life of a higher education professional—be it an academic advisor, a director of a first-year seminar, a professor leading a section of a gateway biology course, or an administrator supervising transition-oriented programs and initiatives—is full of pressures to "get it right." Many of you reading this book will have picked it up, looked at the table of contents, and turned to this chapter in search of answers. We get it. We've been there ourselves. So, if you fall into this group, welcome! We're glad you're here. If you have reached this point having read the previous chapters in order, you also likely are looking for answers to the questions, "What do I do with all of this?" or "What might any of this mean for my day-to-day work?" or "What recommendations do you have for me to even get started?" From the outset of this book's conceptualization, our explicit goal was to provide practical guidance for application of the theoretical perspectives we are advancing.

Whether this chapter is your entry point into the conversation or you have engaged with some combination of the preceding chapters, we encourage you to pay attention to some of the key ideas that have been the focus of our arguments in the book so far as they shape our recommendations for application:

- Transitions represent more than movement, adjustment, development, or socialization.

- Because of transitions' ongoing, everyday nature, they are better thought of in terms of student *becoming*.

- Students enter new academic *communities*, such as college, as novices and learn how to be, do, and think through *participation* with more veteran members of these communities.

- Thus, transition occurs through three modes to which we must attend: community, participation, and becoming.

The Theory–Practice of Transition as Becoming

In this chapter, we will expand on the theory by exploring the connection of the theoretical perspectives with practice. Before describing the structure of the rest of the chapter, we feel it important to say a few things first.

Right away, we must be very clear about what we are not trying to accomplish in this chapter. We are not providing a step-by-step how-to manual for application of the reconsidered theory we have presented. As mentioned in Chapter 1, we believe the most high-impact approaches to supporting transitions have the impact they do because they address the three modes of transition introduced in Chapter 4 (i.e., community, participation, and becoming), not simply because they follow some pre-defined structure such as a first-year seminar, a senior capstone experience, or undergraduate research. In other words, it matters less what we call a transition practice and more that the practice attends to the three modes. One of the main reasons for our reluctance to provide a how-to approach is because transitions, practice, and even theory are contextually situated. It is folly to think we could possibly know of all the unique situations and then present a one-size-fits-all approach that would attend to the nuances and (im)possibilities of community, participation, and becoming on your campuses.

In addition, the split conceptualization of *theory* separate from *practice* might be a useful, but fictitious construction. Theory and practice are "entangled matters" (Taylor & Harris-Evans, 2018, p. 1264), as the presence of one evokes the other. St. Pierre (2016) describes them as inseparable and suggests they could be written as *theorypractice*. We hope our description of the theory has been a more faithful depiction of the practice of transition and that, because of the theory, practice can be more faithfully specified for students' experiences. As a result, we will (roughly) follow the guidance by St. Pierre and refer to this connection as theory–practice throughout this chapter.

Therefore, the suggestions we offer here are focused on providing frameworks for considering the flows between theory and practice. Following advice from Taylor and Harris-Evans (2018), we would encourage you to take these theory–practice frames and experiment with thinking about and doing transition differently on your campuses. This experimentation should focus on creating educational environments "orientated to opening space for students' becomings … and [that] would provide opportunities for students' messy, struggles with knowledge-ing" (Taylor & Harris-Evans, 2018, p. 1264).

With that in mind, we have identified four areas in which practitioners tasked with supporting student transitions will likely find questions about how to apply our perspectives of community, participation, and becoming in transitions:

- Design
- Implementation
- Assessment
- Change toward equity and access

Within each of these four areas, we will present examples, considerations, and questions we think are key for higher education professionals to consider when making decisions about supporting student transitions and for building in community, participation, and becoming. We will offer general perspectives about how to go about answering these questions; however, we must reiterate our position that we cannot answer them for you. Your process of becoming as an educator and institutional actor is one you must enact in your communities and in relationships with your colleagues and students (whom we would encourage you to consider as your colleagues and partners in all of this).

Each section will begin with brief illustrations of application within selected transition programs. We have been intentional in providing a few brief examples. We primarily want to use these as illustrations to set up our discussion of considerations, conversations, and collaborations around the application of reconsidered notions of student transitions. We hope this will spark opportunities to have the same kinds of discussions on your campuses.

Design

We have all been in the position of trying to get a new initiative started. Maybe we are here because we have cultivated an idea from a mere seed, or maybe it is because we have been "voluntold" by our institution's vice provost (or equivalent). If you are in the position of considering the design of programs and initiatives to support student transitions, you are in a position full of opportunity. You have the chance to shape the options around how students can participate, the kinds of relationships that might be present, and the educationally purposeful elements of the initiative.

A Design Example: The STEP Program

To illustrate the theory–practice as it relates to the design of initiatives aimed at supporting students in transition, we present the Second-Year Transformational Experience Program (STEP) at The Ohio State University as an example of how the modes of participation, community, and becoming can be incorporated into the intentional design of a sophomore program (for more details on the program, see Pitstick, 2018).

Students in the STEP program have the opportunity to participate in shaping their own educational experience in partnership with the institution. These students work to map out a proposal for a transformational project that will take place at some point between their sophomore year and their fourth year on campus. Students work with their faculty mentors on the proposal, which includes a budget, an explanation of how they will use up to $2,000 to support their Signature Project, and a personal statement in which they reflect on and explore issues of identity, community, and engagement during their time at Ohio State.

The faculty mentor is a cornerstone of the STEP program (Pitstick, 2018), and the student–faculty relationship both humanizes the faculty and creates a sense among students that they are connected more broadly to the collective faculty at Ohio State. Moreover, community with other students is at the program's core and is built around social and academic connections. This includes activities designed to engage students with aspects of the campus community, the broader community, and one another. Finally, the intentional reflection built into the program includes self-exploration by students about "how all of the aspects of their identities align with their chosen career path" (Pitstick, 2018, p. 99). If there are concerns about alignment, the student and the faculty mentor discuss what changes might be made and what could be done differently to ensure the student can find opportunities for success. All these activities are designed to give students an intentional set of supports as they explore issues of identity, purpose, values, and goals, both academic and personal—in other words, becoming.

Considerations for Design

Several authors have written about the design of programs aimed at supporting college students during transitions, including during the first year (Barefoot et al., 2005; Keup & Petschauer, 2011), the sophomore year (Pitstick, 2018; Schaller, 2018), and the senior year (Henscheid, 2012). Others have offered general design principles, such as Baxter Magolda's (2004) learning partnerships model. Among these recommendations are places where design principles point to opportunities for the intentional incorporation of community, participation, and becoming.

An important principle for the design and development of transition programs is to be intentional in considering and explicit in communicating the roles of the instructor, advisor, or supervisor to members of the community. This is important for newcomers, as well as any continuing students (e.g., peer leaders) or graduate interns who might be participating (Henscheid, 2012). Designing the program as a community of practice should consider faculty and staff in their roles as more experienced members of the community, and also how they will create relationships with students as emergent members as they engage in authentic and meaningful practices of the community. As exemplified in the STEP program, faculty mentors are critical in developing a connection to the institution as well as any academic or disciplinary fields (Pitstick, 2018).

Committing to collaboration and contribution is also critical during design processes, both within the program as well as with other campus partners (Barefoot et al., 2005; Henscheid, 2012; Pitstick, 2018). This commitment is key to building a community with the potential to connect students with the constellation of relationships we will describe further in Chapter 6. It also evokes the idea that the knowledge produced in this environment will be co-constructed, wherein students and institutional professionals are sharing in the potential successes and risks of the educational process, a feature of the learning partnerships model (Baxter Magolda, 2004). Thus, these principles lead to a design of the community as one of belongingness (Schaller, 2018) that balances student independence (Henscheid, 2012) with interdependence in the community (Baxter Magolda, 2004).

Finally, designing a transition program that is open to and encourages becoming could begin with communication with the student and important members of their outside-of-college communities—such as family, friends, faith communities, and employers—the ways students may change during their college experiences (Schaller, 2018). That said, it is important for institutions to understand who students are, what their experiences are like, and to validate them as knowers (Baxter Magolda, 2004; Hallett et al., 2020; Pitstick, 2018; Rendón, 1994; Schaller, 2018). In designing experiences for students, higher education professionals should acknowledge the fluidity present in students' lives (Quinn, 2010; Taylor & Harris-Evans, 2018) and allow for non-linear participation and becoming. Programs should be designed in such a way that students can engage in exploration, (temporary) commitments, discovery about what is not working, and backing up and starting over (Schaller, 2018). Designing for engagement, experimentation, and reflection allows students to expand their knowledge of self, the world, and the self-in-the-world (Schaller, 2018) and increases the potential for transitions to lead to meaningful experiences of becoming.

Key Questions for Design

We believe the following high-level questions are important for building in community, participation, and becoming during the design of transition support programs:

- How can community, participation, and becoming be incorporated into design principles for transition programs?

- How does this new initiative connect students with faculty, advisors, supervisors, peer leaders, and other members of the community in meaningful ways and lead to opportunities for participation?

- How is the initiative's role in the patchwork of campus communities considered? How does it help form community for students that is not solely limited to the community created within the initiative?

- How does this transition program allow for sustained support, not just limited to one particular period, through community, participation, and becoming?

- How are student agency and institutional power dynamics considered in the design of transition programs and initiatives?

- What are some things you can do to move from involvement to participation; narrow community to broader notions of community; knowledge acquisition or social reproduction to becoming?

Implementation

So, you have designed a transition-supporting initiative that attends to the three modes of community, participation, and becoming and offers opportunities for relationships, reflection, and risk. Now that you have to actually execute that plan, what do you do? Or, maybe you would like to implement the theoretical perspectives within the framework of a long-standing transition program.

Because design and implementation walk hand-in-hand, it is impossible to talk about the intended structures and the choices that led to their shaping without some discussion about how they influenced the actual practice. Similarly, it is impossible to talk about how an initiative was carried out without evoking the intention behind the actions. While we acknowledge the distinction between design and implementation might be an artifice, we find it to be a useful one. In this section, we will focus on the goings on in transition programs, or what is required to carry out designs to support transitions.

An Implementation Example: Academic Writing in Undergraduate Research

Howitt et al. (2022) offer a description of an undergraduate research experience (URE) that illustrates how community, participation, and becoming can play an important role in implementing an initiative. This URE is offered in a Bachelor of Advanced Science program at an institution in a large city in Australia that serves the city's suburbs as well as the surrounding region through multiple branch campuses. Students in this program, many of whom are non-traditional, ethnically diverse, and first-generation, are required to undertake three progressive research projects. The first takes place during the second year and requires students to work with an academic supervisor, an experienced member of the academic staff, to identify and critically review a topic connected with the supervisor's research. The URE focuses on the academic writing in the research process and centers the student–faculty relationship as a critical aspect of socializing students to the discipline.

The URE was designed to give students the opportunity to interact with supervisors and peers in the research project. But it does more than just connect students, peers, and faculty; as students work with the other members of the research team to critically review the literature, the emphasis falls more on the practices and process than on the product (Howitt et al., 2022). Students must create a plan, complete a poster presentation, engage in a peer review of the poster, and keep a reflective journal, culminating in their completion of the review itself. This process provides a learning environment where students embark in becoming participants in the scientific community through peer and community interactions.

A key facet of the URE was intentionally building in time and space for students to engage with their disciplinary community (e.g., instructor, peers, scholarly literature) to develop an understanding and acceptance of uncertainty. This required students to move from collecting facts to integrating and crafting narratives, which allowed them to develop their own voice to evaluate and comment on the meaning of complex and often contradictory literature.

In their analysis of how students took on the URE's implementation, Howitt et al. (2022) found that interacting, embodying, and practicing the language of the community helped students become more confident in their membership in disciplinary and academic communities as undergraduate researchers. They noted: "Recognising that they can have valid opinions is an important step for these students in becoming members of the scientific community" (Howitt et al., 2022, p. 10). As a result, the undergraduate researchers experienced epistemological changes. These practices validated the students as learners and knowers and led to greater confidence in their ability to contribute and function as full participants in their new community.

Considerations for Implementation

What can we learn from this example about what we can do when implementing initiatives? In other words, how do we thoughtfully and meaningfully undertake the work we have already designed and planned to better support student becoming in transitions? Although this was previously mentioned during the discussion on design, we turn again to engagement with members of the community through participation. Much has been written about the importance of student–faculty interaction (see Kim & Sax, 2017; Mayhew et al., 2016; Pascarella & Terenzini, 2005). However, the quality of the interaction with faculty matters more than the quantity (Kim & Sax, 2017). When students and faculty work together as co-participants in activities such as (and certainly not limited to) undergraduate research, the opportunities for students to practice and embody the language of the community and be validated as knowers, doers, and thinkers are manifold. This is particularly important, as instructors are key agents for helping students from minoritized backgrounds feel validated as knowers and contributors to the community (Hallett et al., 2020; Lundberg, 2010; Rendón, 1994).

The quality of the interaction in the URE example came about through circumstances favorable for meaningful participation. The students worked alongside their academic supervisors to identify research questions, write the critical review of the literature, present the findings through a poster, and engage in reflection (Howitt et al., 2022). Not only was their interaction with supervisors part of the meaningful and authentic participation, but so was engaging with peers. As students wrestled with new forms of experiencing education, they learned through their interactions with other students in the URE program. What students were not doing, it should be noted, was simply and passively hearing decontextualized bits of information about what it meant to become a member of the scientific and disciplinary community. Instead, they actively contributed and helped develop their voice and sense of self as academics in their own right. It is therefore imperative that transition programs should be implemented as *places to do the things that matter in college, not simply places where we talk about those things*. They might function early on as "rehearsal spaces," as Hatch et al. (2018, p. 139) described, but as students participate more fully, the rehearsal must turn into an authentic performance.

It is also important for institutions to consider how the overall student experience is working in a coordinated and cohesive way to support student transitions across campus. As we stated from the outset in Chapter 1, supporting students in learning and becoming requires an integrated, holistic, and campus-wide approach that engages all stakeholders. Rethinking transitions involves much more than developing and then implementing a single premier program or high-impact intervention. Attending to the multiplicity of on-campus communities a student belongs to is an important way for faculty, student affairs professionals, and administrators to understand and honor the many spaces on campus in which the student is being and becoming. To reiterate, for those who support students in transition, the task is finding ways to bring together a constellation of practices that comprise a community that offers belonging to students by actively inviting them to participate in the process of becoming, on a personal and institutional level.

Key Questions for Implementation

We believe the following high-level questions are important for building in community, participation, and becoming in the intentional implementation of transition support programs:

- How is your transition program operating as a space where students are passive viewers of the college experience, in contrast to creating a rehearsal and performance space for college-going activities?

- How do you work across functional lines to create a coherent experience for students in transition?

- How do we engage with the multiplicity of communities present in students' lives, both on and outside our campuses?

Assessment

To be honest, we approached this part of the section on application with no small amount of apprehension for at least two reasons. First, this is a process in which higher educationalists from all corners of colleges and universities frequently feel overwhelmed and underprepared. For many reasons, including pressures for accountability and justifying resource needs, as well as the orthodoxy around assessment practices (just ask any two of the assessment enthusiasts in your life about how to write a learning outcome, and you'll see what we mean), there is no wonder why people are looking for resources that just tell them how to do it. Second, assessment is frequently built on identification of outcomes and rigid, developmental assumptions of student growth, which do not map neatly onto notions of learning as becoming. In fact, if we followed our theoretical line of reasoning to its conclusion, we might suggest that current forms of assessment should be abandoned completely! Yet, we don't live in that world. The following are ways to consider the tension between the theory we present with the realities of assessment practice as currently constituted.

An Assessment Example: Assessment as Engagement in Undergraduate Business

An apt example of how community, participation, and becoming can appear in an assessment process is found in the practices of the Stillman School of Business at Seton Hall University (for more detail, see Onimus & Strawser, 2021). Faculty at Stillman make use of "assessment panels" to assess student learning as part of their overall program assessment. All undergraduate business students in Stillman take part in an assessment panel either in the second or senior year as a requirement for graduation. Students work in teams of five or six to analyze a case representing concepts relevant to their coursework and their application to a real-world business situation. The students then deliver a 30-minute presentation to a panel of two or three assessors. The assessors are professionals in the industry with at least five years of work experience and, more often than not, are Stillman alumni who have volunteered to stay connected with the school and its activities.

The assessment panels are conducted over a weekend, at times when assessors can participate (Onimus & Strawser, 2021). Novice assessors are paired with veteran assessors to use rubrics to evaluate students' presentations on each of the competency areas. After the presentations, assessors engage directly with the students to probe further on their learning and how they took part in teamwork, collaboration, and the process for completing the project. After the presentation and question-and-answer session, assessors coach students on how they can improve, both with oral feedback in the moment and later with written feedback.

This approach to assessment offers several benefits, as listed by Onimus & Strawser (2021). First, assessors provide students with developmental feedback connected to current trends in the discipline. Students participate in a learning process throughout the evaluation and "often view courses that incorporate [alumni and industry professional] participation as more impactful than those that are delivered solely by academics" (Onimus & Strawser, 2021, p. 157). Further, this approach has positive impacts for the program curriculum; the feedback helps program organizers know what the industry is hoping graduates will be able to know and do, and how well students are being prepared for their future professional lives. Finally, engaging these stakeholders improves information sharing and strengthens relationships between alumni, students, the program, and Stillman.

Considerations for Assessment

The theory–practice perspectives outlined throughout the book point to realities that must be acknowledged when engaging in the assessment of transition programs. Assessment, like learning and becoming, is not only socially situated but is a social practice (Wall et al., 2014). Social practices are complex and situational; the same practices employed in different circumstances will lead to different results. Wall et al. (2014) explain that social practices, including assessment, are "developed through learning in practice, through mentoring and experiential learning rather than from mastery of a set of abstract knowledge" (p. 10). This might sound similar to some of the concepts we presented in Chapter 3 (assessment competence is developed through a process of situated learning). As a result, we are reluctant to offer concrete advice for creating specific learning outcomes and the associated methods for measuring or identifying them. This is something you must establish for the students on your campus while navigating the social realities present at your institution and within your students' communities. That said, we recommend the following as considerations when engaging in assessment.

Assessment, as it is concerned with institutional self-awareness and change, is a natural fit for the conversation of becoming. Yet, what should we consider in the theory–practice of assessment of transition programs? To start, we recommend thinking of assessment as a process of organizational learning (Young, 2018). This perspective requires acknowledgement that our transition support programs are in a state of flux and becoming, and this is apparent through the assessment process. When those responsible for transition programs embrace an organizational learning framework, they are intentionally learning and actively engaged in processes of change alongside students. As learning organizations, transition programs must be engaged in double-loop learning (Argyris & Schön, 1996). This requires educators to engage in dialogue with students and other stakeholders and to take risks by engaging in vulnerability and interdependence (Swing & Ross, 2016; Young, 2018).

We must continually challenge our assumptions about the student experience, monitoring and adapting our understanding of the experiences of students who are in transition. As we do so, assessment is an important way to demonstrate institutional integrity and create co-agentic spaces, as discussed in Chapter 2. In the Stillman example, the school engaged in co-participation with key stakeholders in assessing its undergraduate business program. The Stillman faculty involved current and former students in organizational learning as partners, providing the benefit of making students stakeholders in their own education.

As with any social practice, we must attend to the power dynamics at play with transition and how we assess it. We have mentioned previously that the terms of transition are frequently set by the institution and those who hold power (Kitchen et al., 2019; Quinn, 2010). This dynamic shows up in assessment, as it is inherently political (Henning & Roberts, 2016; Skolnik, 2010; Wall et al., 2014). However, assessment can be operationalized as an ethical and valuing social practice (for more on this, see Heiser et al., 2017; Henning & Lundquist, 2019; Wall et al., 2014) that attends to the social and political positions it occupies. For example, we would do well to ask:

- Who is setting the objectives for student learning and becoming in our transition programs?

- How are we partnering with students in the interpretation of assessment results?

- What cross-campus stakeholders are we not including in our assessment?

- How are we centering student community, participation, and becoming in the change processes connected to our assessment?

Such questions encourage institutional actors to consider their assessment roles and processes through the lens of co-agentic and ethical practice, and to frame assessment as pedagogy, or organizational self-reflection, critique, and learning (Wall et al., 2014). In other words, when we engage students, faculty, and student affairs staff together as co-participants in ethical assessment practices, assessment starts to flower into a form of institutional becoming.

Key Questions for Assessment

We believe the following high-level questions are important for building in community, participation, and becoming in the assessment of transition support programs:

- How can we move toward assessment of student learning in transitions in ways that honor the fluidity of student transitions and therefore embrace a socially contextualized understanding of the educational effectiveness of our work?

- What do assessment and organizational learning look like when we operate from a paradigm of participation and situated learning?

- How can we recognize and attend to issues of institutional and student agency in setting and evaluating objectives for students during transition? What insights does this give us into the power and politics inherent in common formats of learning outcomes assessment in higher education?

- How do we center the students' agency within institutional interests?

- How do our assessment efforts figure into institutional becoming?

Change Toward Equity and Access

Throughout the book, we have referred to the role of power, structure, and historical oppression relating to groups during their transitions to college, including racially minoritized, low-income, and first-generation students. We hold that our theoretical position opens considerations for how we attend to issues of equity and access. Moreover, higher education professionals must find ways to not only be open to the changes necessary to improve transitions for these students, but also to be actively engaged in the change.

An Example of Change Toward Equity and Access: Self-Directed Placement in Developmental Education

The *Self-Directed Placement* approach to developmental education, developed at the Community College of Baltimore County (CCBC), offers an excellent model for how transition-as-becoming and the modes of community, participation, and becoming appear in a process of change toward improved equity and access (for more details, see Messer et al., 2022). Faculty teaching developmental English courses at CCBC noticed that a disproportionate number of the students in developmental sections were students of color. More than two-thirds of African American students were required to take at least one developmental course to fulfill the CCBC English requirement, compared with fewer than half of the White students beginning at CCBC. Similarly, part-time students were at least twice as likely to be placed into developmental education as their full-time counterparts. Driven by the idea that "placement is destiny" (Messer et al., 2022, p. 86), this disparity became the impetus for change.

To improve equity among the incoming students, a faculty committee at CCBC engaged in serious conversations to reform placement processes there (Messer et al., 2022). A core value of the committee was building a strong sense of belonging and confidence from the start of students' experiences at CCBC. Moreover, they wanted students to feel that the institution recognized and valued the experiences and strengths of students from different backgrounds, including culturally and linguistically diverse communities, as well as students who were entering college after time away from formal education. The committee wanted to create "exploratory vistas" (Messer et al., 2022, p. 88) for students to be able to see themselves as successful at CCBC and beyond.

As a result, the committee intentionally sought to eliminate the use of a placement score, attributable to

- the inauthenticity of a simple score relative to many of the communities and social contexts important to students,

- the lack of a score's predictive power relative to success in college,

- the reality that placement scores are founded in a system of inequity that systematically disadvantages members of cultural groups, and

- recognition of placement scores as a tool that undermines student confidence and creates negative interactions with spaces where they seek (and have been promised) belonging (Messer et al., 2022).

The committee's goal was to create spaces where (a) students' agency and self-efficacy were central to their own educational experience and (b) students could be partners with the institution in shaping it.

The committee designed a self-directed placement practice for English in which a student could engage in conversation based on guided reflections driven by their self-reported confidence and previous experiences in English (Messer et al., 2022). Students were key stakeholders in the reform process, and their feedback was sought throughout the design, piloting, and implementation of the change. The proposed change was, as one would expect, seen as overly risky and met with skepticism, concern, or resistance by partners from many entities on CCBC's campus, including student services, advising, information technology, and even faculty colleagues in academic literacy. Multiple rounds of pilots, strategic planning conversations, campus visits from consultants, and assessments offering proof of concept provided space to allay those apprehensions.

Considerations for Change toward Equity and Access

The self-directed placement approach at CCBC illustrates how community, participation, and becoming are intricately connected with issues of equity and access. First, institutional leaders saw that their academic community's distribution of racial composition signaled an inequitable apportionment of access to credit-bearing coursework. Because greater shares of African American students were being placed in developmental courses, they were deviated from full participation in the academic curriculum. As part of their response to this issue, leaders sought to attend to other hallmarks of community: namely, student sense of belonging and valuing student backgrounds and strengths, including cultural and linguistic diversity.

In addition, redress included greater participation of students as stakeholders in the reform process. Students were intentionally included and validated as experts, meaning-makers, and contributors to the institutional change process. Their involvement did not end there; student co-participation in the placement practice was codified, and students partnered with the institution in charting their educational course. Student becoming was embodied throughout this process. As students were made participants in the decision-making process of the academic community, they were exposed to the exploratory vistas desired by the committee and realized greater self-efficacy and agency.

The example from CCBC illustrates not only how the modes of transition are at play when a campus policy is changed to improve equity and access, but also points to the idea that issues of transition are fundamentally concerned with equity and inclusion. For instance, in the CCBC case, what signal is sent when a student is admitted but they are immediately told they are not ready for the very communities and practices to which they have gained access? This problem interacts with messages from the student's membership in communities that society continues to oppress. "Students from marginalized groups—students of color, first-generation students—may interpret minor setbacks in particular ways. For example, they may view these relatively minor interactions as indicative of the fairness of the higher education systems or institutions" (Jabbar et al., 2021, p. 22). Jury et al. (2017) stressed, "higher education is far from being a culturally neutral environment for low SES students, notably because the system is 'built and organized according to taken for granted, middle- and upper-class cultural norms, unwritten codes, or 'rules of the game'" (p. 18).

So, how do we de-neutralize the way we think about transitions and create opportunities for community, participation, and becoming in our practices that promote greater equity and access? One promising approach to de-neutralizing transitions is to build equity-minded (McNair et al., 2020) and race-conscious (Harper, 2009) practices. Equity-mindedness represents a critical awareness of the structural inequality and demands actions to change systems that uphold institutional racism (Bensimon, 2018). It seeks the achievement of parity of student achievement based on race, which is cast against the omnipresence of whiteness as the underpinning of institutions of higher education (McNair et al., 2020). One basic approach to engaging in equity-minded practice is to monitor students' participation in high-quality and high-impact transition programs and then to disaggregate by race and ethnicity, as well as by other key demographics connected to structural inequality (e.g., gender, ability, sexuality, income, parental education, age). Faculty at CCBC demonstrated this equity-mindedness as they considered the participation rates of Black students in their developmental education sections. Moreover, equity-mindedness requires a commitment to understand the structural barriers to accessing the transition programs themselves, as well as any opportunities for participation, community, and becoming that students might be missing out on as they are held in positions of marginality.

Similarly, race-conscious practices require that we, as educators, accept the responsibility for the success of racially minoritized students on our campus (Harper, 2009). They also require that we "acknowledge qualitative differences in the experiences of racial minority students" (Harper, 2009, p. 42). This requires institutions and their actors to become open to the ways of knowing and experiencing the world these students bring with them. In Chapter 2, we highlighted a handful of studies showing that transitions for students from groups historically underserved by higher education require those students to fall in line with social roles determined by dominant groups and to give up familiar ways of knowing, doing, and being. So, the questions that face institutions of higher education wishing to engage in change toward greater equity and access include:

- How do our current practices create real opportunity for students from minoritized racial and ethnic backgrounds to participate in our communities on campus?

- How have previous educational environments signaled to students that the participation of members of their racial or ethnic communities was not valued, and what kinds of signals is our current environment sending?

- To what extent are we asking students to align their visions of their future selves with ours?

- Who gets to have agency in the negotiation of pathways toward becoming that future self?

The answer to these questions is not of trivial concern. To understand transitions in the ways we have argued in this book (i.e., students entering as new members into a community of practice that holds powerful potential for transformation and becoming), those of us who work as institutional actors must hold to a high ethical standard. We must continue to ask ourselves:

- Who has access to our communities, and how do they become members of them?

- Who has been afforded the opportunity to participate in the authentic activities of our communities, and what does participation mean for them?

- When students participate in communities of practice, how does that shape and contribute to their becoming, and how do their contributions shape the becoming of the institution?

These questions are at the heart of transition programs—the primary vehicle for achieving and maintaining equity and access.

Key Questions for Change Toward Equity and Access

We believe the following high-level questions are important for attending to equity and access within community, participation, and becoming in transition support programs:

- How is equity-mindedness central to community, participation, and becoming in our transition programs and initiatives?

- How can our efforts to support transition not be centered only on the students who are most easily identified in the transitions most convenient to the institution?

- How can our transition programs create "exploratory vistas" (Messer et al., 2022, p. 88) for more students than just those who come from economically or socially privileged backgrounds?

- What is the appetite or willingness on campus or within any given transition program to consider changing the ways to understand and frame transition as equity-minded and race-conscious?

Conclusion

We hope these examples, considerations, and questions open pathways for imagining, discussing, and experimenting as you think about applying the modes of community, participation, and becoming to your practice situated on your campus and with your students. To be completely frank, we have seen examples of the theory–practice described in this book in many more places than we had the space to share in this chapter. However, we would encourage you to avoid the temptation to seek them out merely to try to copy their approaches wholesale.

Instead, we would repeat our urging that you take these theory–practice frames and experiment with thinking about and doing transition differently on your campuses. Experimentation likely includes all four of the areas of application included in this chapter. Before an idea is implemented in practice, there must be some design behind the thought. The influence or effectiveness of an implemented approach requires some form of assessment. Accordingly, assessment and evaluation should lead to deeper understanding of design and implementation of initiatives. And through it all, practical approaches to supporting transitions must carry attention to equity and access through design, implementation, and assessment.

Experimentation evokes an understanding that application, much like transition, is best understood as a learning process and not an end goal. As you engage with the theory–practice of transition, you (hopefully) will learn from each attempt, and each engagement will lead to a theory-in-practice that represents a new point of view from which you can expand the experimentation. We encourage you to think about how community, participation, and becoming are situated in your institutional policy or research contexts. Similarly, we challenge you to think about these three modes of transition as you develop, implement, and evaluate equity-minded approaches. Along the way, you will inevitably encounter examples of the flux, movement, and tensions of stability and instability that exemplify becoming.

Admittedly, that all might sound a bit vague and lofty, so in the next chapter, we will offer three avenues for starting your experimentation with applying the theory–practice represented in the modes of community, participation, and becoming. As we present ways the three modes can be expressed through relationships, reflection, and risk, we encourage you to think about how these "three Rs" can help students as they become meaningful participants in academic communities of practice. We also encourage you to consider how these might point to what could be done in your context to bring the theory–practice to life.

Crucial Considerations

The following questions can help guide or initiate conversations with key partners on your campus or in your research networks and serve as starting points for rethinking transition theory–practice:

- How can attention to community, participation, and becoming lead to greater equity and access during the designing of initiatives for supporting transitions?

- How can attention to community, participation, and becoming lead to greater equity and access during implementation of those initiatives?

- How can attention to community, participation, and becoming in assessment of initiatives for supporting transitions lead to greater equity and access?

- How is equity-mindedness central to community, participation, and becoming in our transition programs and initiatives? How can experimentation in the application of theory–practice of transition increase capacity for equity-minded and race-conscious approaches?

Chapter 6 | Practical Starting Points for Experimentation with Becoming: Relationships, Reflection, and Risk

We hope our discussion of theory–practice in Chapter 5 helped you begin to envision how you might engage in experimentation with the modes of *community, participation*, and *becoming*. As a reminder, we see the process of supporting students in transition as most effective when approached from a *becomingist* perspective, in which the goal is to design educational environments that open the door for transformative learning in transitions. As we continue to pivot from a focus on theory to thinking about what these ideas mean for practice, it seems useful to provide additional support and ideas for potential starting or entry points in this process.

Ultimately, our aim with this chapter is to continue to intentionally entangle theory and practice by providing additional practical recommendations, while also illuminating the interrelationships between community, participation, and becoming. Viewing these three modes as working together in concert is critical. After all, there can be no participation without community, no community without some aspect of becoming, and no real hope of experiencing becoming without the opportunity to participate with others in a community. Indeed, to fully appreciate the role of community, participation, and becoming in transitions, it is important to view these modes as integrated parts of a unified and holistic framework, with one instantiating the others.

As we discussed practical starting points for applying the three modes toward improving the experiences of students in transition, we frequently found our conversations returning to three key considerations for the work of supporting transitions: *relationships, reflection,* and *risk.* We have chosen to focus on these elements because they serve as helpful entry points in our effort to think more carefully about the applications and implications of the theory–practice of transitions as becoming. In what follows, we use them as a sort of window to illuminate how community, participation, and becoming show up in the work of supporting students in transition.

Relationships

The past four decades of research on college success have provided abundant evidence that relationships are at the heart of learning and play a critical role in the experiences of students in transition (e.g., Astin, 1977; Light, 2001; Mayhew et al., 2016; Schreiner et al., 2020a; Tinto, 2012). When students participate in meaningful activities with others in their community, whether via a useful connection with a fellow post-traditional student who is also balancing college and a career, supportive guidance from an academic advisor, or mentoring by a faculty member, they become different types of learners. Further, there is clear evidence that supportive learning relationships have an outsized impact on students from populations that historically have been excluded or marginalized on our campuses (Kezar & Maxey, 2014), including first-generation students, students of color, low-income students, and neurodiverse students (Baldwin et al., 2020; Cohen, 2022; Sisk et al., 2018; Yeager et al., 2016). In short, one of the defining features of environments that offer opportunities for community, participation, and becoming is that they are *relationship rich* (Felten & Lambert, 2020). This involves more than simply placing students in proximity to faculty, staff, and peers and expecting positive outcomes to result. Instead, institutions need to carefully consider the nature, quality, and function of the relationships they work to broker for students. These relationships are the backbone of the communities of which students are a part, and they enhance the learning possible through meaningful participation in community practices.

When Our Goal Is Becoming, the Purpose and Nature of Students' Relationships Shift

Regardless of the perspective or metaphor for transitions that an individual practitioner or institution more generally might adopt (see Table 2.4), relationships will be a visible part of their efforts to support students in transition. However, the purpose and nature of these relationships will vary depending on how we define transitions. For example, when transitions are viewed through the lens of movement or adjustment, relationships with academic advisors simply facilitate the transfer of information from an institutional authority to an uninformed student. The purpose of the relationship is to ensure adjustment to institutional expectations, alignment with institutional policy, or fit with institutional culture. Similarly, when we define transition in terms of individual development, relationships with peers offer social support or foster intellectual or emotional development by providing exposure to diverse perspectives.

Relationships clearly contribute to these sorts of outcomes and position students for a positive transition experience. However, when we shift our focus and define transitions as a process of becoming, we begin to see that students' relationships serve purposes beyond adjustment, orientation, fit, or development. In fact, these relationships might be more than just vehicles for acquiring knowledge, developing discrete skills, or fulfilling course-level or programmatic outcomes. Indeed, we argue that relationships are critical outcomes in and of themselves.

For example, Bryce's institution (Brigham Young University, BYU) is in the midst of developing and piloting a new first-year seminar course required of all first-year students as part of BYU's general education requirements. Throughout the curriculum-development process, institutional leaders placed great emphasis on crafting a reading list for the course that would seemingly ensure new students had learned and understood the ideas and perspectives deemed critical for success at BYU. However, assessment data gathered from students, peer leaders, and faculty participating in two early pilots of the course has provided strong evidence that the single most important outcome of the course are the relationships new students have developed with the members of their first-year seminar community. While course readings and assessments have deepened students' understanding of BYU's institutional mission and introduced them to campus resources, students overwhelmingly report that the course's greatest benefit is the resulting relationships. This has been particularly important for students who, for a variety of reasons (e.g., childcare responsibilities, work commitments, long commutes to campus) do not have the time to establish relationships outside of class.

Not only have these relationships in the first-year seminar contributed to powerful forms of community, but they have also facilitated meaningful participation, as students have engaged together in attending campus events, collaborating on group projects, and engaging with faculty (both in and outside of class). This has provided invaluable insight for institutional leaders charged with refining the course design and demonstrated that an intentional focus on relationships offers both community and participation for first-year students at BYU.

This example also helps to illustrate that becoming requires more than just acquiring isolated units of knowledge. Becoming is a community experience, and it is the relationships with others in our community that are best suited to offer opportunities to experience this transformative growth.

When becoming is our goal, we also begin to ask different sorts of questions about the role of relationships in transitions: How might we structure relationships in ways that foster connections with new communities? How can we approach relationships to preserve students' ties with previous communities or communities outside our institution? Or what sorts of relationships will provide access to powerful participation with peers and professors?

By foregrounding becoming in our practical efforts to support transitions, we begin to see the fundamental purpose of relationships is to provide students with (a) access to membership in key communities that will support their growth and (b) opportunities to participate in the practices of that community that will help them experience becoming.

Further, the integrated view of *transitions as becoming* and *legitimate peripheral participation*, established in Chapter 3, helps clarify that the benefits of becoming are not limited to individual students in transition, whether they be first-year students, students entering a new discipline or department, or students transitioning out of college into a career. One of the things that excites us most about a practical approach to transitions as becoming is that it prompts questions and design decisions relative to curricula and programming that position everyone in the community for becoming and transformation. Indeed, when an institution prioritizes relationships as a way to offer community and participation for students in transition, it catalyzes innovations, program improvements, and policy shifts that start to look like *institutional becoming*. In short, when we focus on relationships as a means of becoming, everyone wins.

When Our Goal Is Becoming, We Think Differently About Whom Students Should Connect With (And Stay Connected With)

First-year seminars are an interesting context in which to consider who we bring students into contact with during their college transitions. For example, a typical first-year seminar grounded in goals of adjustment or development might inadvertently limit students' relationships to an unnecessarily small and relatively one-dimensional community of other first-year peers and an adjunct instructor whose less expensive labor protects the time of full-time faculty. While this community might provide an intimate and comfortable environment that feels safe and supportive, what a new student really needs is a *constellation of relationships* with folks beyond the narrow community of the seminar class. This might include faculty members, academic advisors, more experienced peers, or librarians, to name a few. Consequently, one entry point into the work of improving first-year students' experiences on a particular campus would be identifying members of the campus community who can engage with new students in activities, conversations, and practices that invite them to become part of the broader learning community at the institution. Of course, a small, intimate class can be an important experience for students in transition and provide a means of connection in the classroom, but we argue that students' community and connections should not be limited to their peers and professor in the seminar.

The same can be said for the variety of other transitions that students experience during college. As students progress beyond the first year, their need for expanded relational networks grows. The sophomore year experience illustrates this well. For students navigating the transitions typically associated with the second year of college, relationships with academic advisors, faculty members, and peers who share the same academic interests become increasingly important. These relationships serve to help students strengthen their major certainty, join communities associated with their academic interests, and engage in high-impact practices that open the door for continued progress toward graduate school or career goals (e.g., undergraduate research, internships, study abroad; Hartman & Young, 2021; Perez, 2020; Schreiner et al., 2020b).

Similarly, as students approach their senior year and post-college transitions, their identities continue to evolve as they begin to see themselves less as college students and more like apprentice journalists, scientists, teachers, or managers, to name a few options. Consequently, to facilitate and support this process of becoming, institutions can prioritize helping students establish relationships beyond institutional walls with potential employers, professional mentors working in students' fields, alumni who can broker professional opportunities, or faculty members in potential graduate school programs (Louis & Hulme, 2020). Of course, this all takes time, which is a privilege not enjoyed by many of today's college students. One critical role academic advisors and others can play—especially for students balancing full-time work with one or two classes each semester—is helping them reflect on the communities and relationships already in their network and seek out mentors and advocates among those existing relationships.

Continuing this topic, considering transitions as opportunities for becoming also decreases the likelihood of students being pressured to engage in *relational pruning* by abandoning prior relationships that higher education professionals frequently and erroneously believe might threaten their success. This happens most often with first-generation students, post-traditional students, international students, and students from other under-resourced communities. In these cases, academic advisors, faculty mentors, and others might be prone to subtly encourage students to cut ties with prior communities that could be distractions or "get in the way" of their full immersion in the college experience (Morton, 2019). Of course, some degree of separation from prior relationships and communities is always involved when students experience transitions. But calls to abandon these existing connections are based on a deficit view that fails to acknowledge the value of community cultural wealth and maligns marginalized communities as "places full of cultural poverty disadvantages" (Yosso, 2005, p. 69). A focus on becoming can help us better recognize that all students, regardless of background, come to college as knowers and with valuable pre-existing funds of knowledge and relational networks that can serve as assets across students' many transition experiences (Daddow, 2016; Moll et al., 1992; Tazewell, 2022).

In summary, the sorts of relationships we have described here are ideal vehicles to provide students with community connections and opportunities to participate in the practices of their campus. This participation opens the door for students to both become authentic members of the academic community and become more fully developed versions of themselves as individuals.

Reflection

Reflection is a particularly important consideration because of its power to integrate and deepen the identity-forming learning and becoming that are possible during times of transition. Though Lave and Wenger were right—participating with others in the meaningful practices of a community of practice does facilitate becoming—we feel it helpful to add a Deweyan spin to the framework of situated learning. We suggest that this becoming is more powerful when accompanied by regular reflection on this *participation in the practices of the community* and the *way one is experiencing becoming* (see Dewey, 1933, for an in-depth discussion of the role of reflection in deepening the learning that comes with experience).

Reflection Can Bring Connection and Cohesion to Community, Participation, and Becoming

Reflection is closely tied to issues of community because members of students' various communities (e.g., faculty, academic advisors, peer educators, parents, religious leaders) are often best positioned to support student reflection by encouraging (and sometimes requiring) them to make meaning of their participation, both formally and informally. Additionally, community members can serve as a powerful audience for students' formal reflections and provide a more authentic participatory experience that deepens students' learning and becoming. In fact, while writing this section, it occurred to us that the act of co-authoring this book has been a powerful reflective experience for us—one that has not just clarified our thinking but also facilitated our becoming in unique ways.

Further, without you, the reader, as an audience or community for our reflection, this experience would have been fundamentally different and much less likely to result in our becoming better teachers, researchers, practitioners, and humans. While we have been talking together about these ideas since 2017, it wasn't until we began to formally reflect—and share our reflections with real audiences via conference presentations, articles submitted for publication in higher education journals, and now this book—that our thinking began to crystallize and deepen. Similarly, for students, reflection with members of various campus communities is a powerful form of participation that contributes to becoming.

Engaging in reflection seems to be relatively common at the conclusion of students' experience, as it helps them recognize the kinds of learners, thinkers, and doers they have become through the sum of their educational experiences (Gardner & Van der Veer, 1998; Henscheid et al., 2019; Louis & Hulme, 2020; Parrish, 2009). However, this sort of reflection can also be an important part of college students' early experiences. By allowing students to reflect on and identify the skills, experiences, and interests they bring with them to college, as well as how their new community and relationships can support them in further growing and becoming, reflection can serve as a welcoming rite of passage. In other words, reflection provides opportunities for students to engage in integrative and applied learning across the entirety of their college experience. In short, it both honors who students have become and helps them chart a path forward toward future becoming.

Reflection Can Help Expand Community, Participation, and Becoming

This brings us back to an issue we have raised at various points in the book about inherent tensions associated with transition experiences. We feel this is important to highlight, as the act of grappling with and negotiating these tensions via reflection provides some of the most impactful opportunities for becoming. For example, for a first-generation student from an indigenous community who leaves home to attend college, reflection will play a vital role in their becoming. At some point in their experience, the student will be faced with the tension between "moving up and moving out" of their previous community and moving forward in their learning, while maintaining ties to the people, places, and values associated with home (e.g., Fish & Syed, 2018; Griffin & Gilbert, 2015; McHenry-Sorber & Swisher, 2020; Morton, 2019; O'Shea, 2015; Rodriguez & Mallinckrodt, 2021).

Similarly, a post-traditional student returning to college after their first career in order to pursue a "second act" will benefit from reflection. Specifically, faculty and other mentors could engage this student in reflecting on how their previous learning, community memberships, identities, and skills can position them for new forms of becoming in the communities and relationships that will emerge from their new experiences. Rather than seeing this rich set of prior experiences as "baggage," reflection could help the student feel a sense of membership and connection in their new communities, as well as identify opportunities for them to contribute and participate in ways unavailable to their traditional peers. Only through thoughtful reflection—and certainly support through the relationships in both communities—will the student discover ways they can participate and maintain membership in those communities.

Finally, we feel it important to point out how reflection can contribute to becoming at the institutional level. Campuses committed to becoming will provide students with voice, ownership, and opportunities to contribute by inviting them to reflect, in public ways, about their experiences in transition, a form of co-agentic practice we first referenced in Chapter 2. Not only will this reflective participation deepen students' experience of community and belonging, it also will provide institutions with invaluable feedback relative to the ways they can refine and improve how they support students in transition and offer opportunities for becoming.

Risk

In Chapter 1 we asserted that college is made up of a series of interconnected transitions and that transitions are integral to the process of learning and becoming. Because we see learning and transitions as linked, we love this description of learning from the instructional designer Patrick Parrish: "Learning is always a perilous undertaking— one in which the learner voluntarily enters a situation that challenges current beliefs and concepts" (2009, p. 516). We agree—learning, becoming, and transitions always entail some degree of risk because, by definition, a transition is a time when we encounter some form of newness or unfamiliarity. Interestingly, transitions programming is often aimed at easing or smoothing students' transition experience or minimizing certain "risky" aspects. This is particularly true when transitions are viewed as processes of movement or adjustment. Clearly, we have a moral obligation to identify and remove barriers that systematically deny particular student populations access to full participation in the community of higher education. However, supporting students in transition does not imply removing all risk or shielding students from any feelings of vulnerability.

As with both relationships and reflection, considering the role of risk in transitions provides yet another glimpse into the interrelationships between the modes of community, participation, and becoming. You'll recall from Chapter 3 that we find value in seeing new students as *peripheral participants* in the communities that make up our college campuses. Further, as we have discussed in previous chapters, students in transition learn about college most effectively, not by being kept in marginalizing "holding spaces," disconnected from the rest of the campus community, but by *experiencing* a developmentally appropriate slice of the practices, conversations, resources, and relationships that offer opportunities for authentic engagement and contribution.

So, in service of our exploration of the role of *risk* in transitions, it is worthwhile to discuss a few relevant etymologies for just a moment.

The words *experience* and *experiment* both come from the same Latin root (*experior*), which means to test, to try, to find out, or to endure. When we adopt the paradigm of transitions as opportunities to become, students' experiences can then be seen as opportunities to test out, try on for size, or experiment with new ways of being. It's through this process of experimenting with various future or provisional selves that students experience the ongoing process of becoming as they navigate the various transitions that make up college. But this experimentation doesn't come without risk. In fact, the word *peril* comes from the same Latin root as *experience* and *experiment*. The best experiences—the ones that really position us for growth—always involve some degree of risk or peril. This position has important implications for transitions that we discuss next.

Student Participation Must Be Connected to the Community's Success or Failure

One common element of nearly every practical example we have shared of programs or initiatives that support becoming has been an invitation to students to shift from being passive observers or consumers of experiences to respected or valued contributors to the practices of a particular community. When students have meaningful opportunities to contribute, whether in a classroom, residence hall, research lab, or some other sub-community on campus, their participation doesn't just keep them occupied and out of trouble or help them learn something useful. When we invite students to contribute to significant workings of the institution, we have real skin in the game, and we come to actually depend on student participation for the success of the practices of the community.

Undergraduate research is a prime example of this form of participation. As faculty members and students work together on a research project, not only are students placed in a situation in which they adjust to college-level learning or develop into more skilled learners, they become part of a real community of learners by participating in something that matters for everyone involved. Along the way, the student is much more likely to invest significant time and energy in their learning, interact with faculty and peers in meaningful ways, and have real-world opportunities to apply their learning. They are also more likely to rise to meet the high expectations associated with being part of a research team, receive frequent feedback on their work, have opportunities to reflect on and integrate their learning, and benefit from the accountability that comes with this type of participation.

For some readers, the preceding list might sound familiar, and it should: It is the list of characteristics of high-impact practices identified by AAC&U (Kuh & O'Donnell, 2013). It should be no surprise that experiences meeting these criteria are associated with significant educational benefits for the students who participate in them, particularly those from demographic groups historically underserved by higher education. We argue that these high-impact educational practices increase student retention and student engagement because they are not just focused on helping students move through college, adjust to new expectations, or experience personal development. Rather, they invite students to become full participants in the institution's most meaningful work: engaging in research, traveling abroad to connect classroom learning with hands-on experiences, collaborating with others to solve problems and share learning, and more.

Again, the magic of these sorts of experiences is that they, in some form or another, involve a degree of risk and authenticity. The success of the student and of the broader endeavor are based in part on the degree the student can apply their knowledge and skill to the task at hand. Additionally, this "success" extends well beyond the awarding of an arbitrary number of points or even a summative course grade. The stakes are higher because the audience for the demonstration of students' learning consists of not just classmates and teachers, but peers and colleagues who are offering membership in an extramural community directly connected to students' future goals and plans. These contexts, with their sense of risk and urgency around learning, offer rich opportunities for students to experience becoming.

The educative value of embracing and offering experiences that include productive risk is powerfully highlighted in an exploration of the characteristics of senior students who reported high degrees of thriving in their transition out of college (Louis & Hulme, 2020). Researchers used purposeful sampling to identify 22 recent recipients of the Truman Scholarship who would be graduating from college within a few weeks of their initial interview with researchers. This prestigious scholarship is awarded to students who have demonstrated high levels of academic achievement, significant leadership potential, and a commitment to ongoing leadership through their careers in public service.

Researchers reported that the most common and notable characteristic among these students was their willingness to embrace uncertainty, accept failure as a learning opportunity, and even deliberately seek out experiences that allowed them to confront discomfort as they developed new skills and abilities. Further, study participants often described how their tolerance for productive risk and uncertainty had been fueled by individual faculty members and a broader institutional culture that both modeled and encouraged measured risk-taking as part of the process of learning, becoming, and preparing for post-graduation opportunities (Louis & Hulme, 2020).

Student Participation Must Involve Risk for Faculty, Staff, and Institutional Leaders

The productive risk Louis and Hulme (2020) highlighted should not be limited only to students. Ultimately, *shared risk* is at the very heart of what it means to be in a co-agentic community. Consider: If there is no risk, can there be interdependence? If there is no interdependence, can there (really) be a community?

For student participation to open the door for becoming during times of transition, the educative vulnerability and risk that characterize high-impact transition experiences need to extend to faculty, staff, advisors, and institutional leaders. As educators and professionals, we must frequently step back to reflect on what the stakes are for us in terms of the transition programs and experiences we are designing to support students. One practice we highly encourage is a periodic "risk audit," in which campus leaders examine the ways they are supporting students in transition and ask how many of these programs, initiatives, courses, or experiences place themselves as leaders in the position of having a real stake in student success. As part of this reflective audit, leaders might ask questions like, "If a student really failed in this particular experience, would it have any impact on me, my department, or the institution?" Or "Is the risk involved through participation a shared risk, or is the risk borne largely by the student?"

Similarly, reflecting on the extent that we share the burden of risk with students in transition also helps to reveal how well we are attending to the three modes of transition introduced in Chapter 4. First, shared risk with students in transition signals that we have begun to provide real membership in our *communities*—not just the safe communities on the margins of the institution that have no real bearing on our work or priorities. But rather, our classrooms, our labs, our research groups, our university committees, and any other spaces where students are participating alongside us in the shared work of learning and teaching. Second, as highlighted in the previous section, inviting students to participate with us in the core functions of our institutions is a sign that we are offering transformative opportunities for participation. Finally, though transition work is not about making students over in our own image, we do have the responsibility to provide access to the same "person-forming properties" (Barnett, 2009, p. 435) of experience that have contributed to our own *becoming* as members of our campus and disciplinary communities. As described previously, this happens most powerfully when we create co-agentic spaces and invite students into positions as contributors and co-participants in the same sorts of activities we are involved in as faculty, staff, and advisors—risky business indeed.

A Practical Example: Relationships, Reflection, and Risk in Undergraduate Research

As we wrapped up the initial writing of this chapter, Bryce stumbled upon a simple example of how relationships, reflection, and risk show up in an increasingly common high-impact practice: undergraduate research. We hope this brief discussion of a practice that is relatively familiar to readers will help illustrate both the utility of these "three Rs" as practical starting points for rethinking transitions, and the interrelationships between the modes of transition introduced in earlier chapters.

The context for the example was the college of social sciences at BYU. The college sponsored an undergraduate research conference highlighting various research projects proposed and conducted by undergraduate students, with support from faculty mentors. As Bryce walked through the space where students were sharing their research posters and engaging with conference attendees, he saw relationships, reflection, and risk on display in interesting ways. Much like what one would see in graduate education, students had formed true collegial *relationships* with faculty members to explore together research questions that had been framed by the students but were connected to faculty members' broader research agendas. Additionally, *reflection* was at the heart of the conference, being powerfully illustrated both by the highly professional posters developed by students as well as the conversations between students and faculty milling about in the open presentation space. Finally, the whole undertaking involved a healthy degree of *risk* for both students and their faculty mentors. They had invested time, energy, and often research funding in exploring these questions and like with all good research, they had leaned into the productive uncertainty that comes with scholarly inquiry.

This short description also highlights how all three modes of transition we introduced in Chapter 4 can come together to provide an opportunity for becoming. Students at the conference were participating in the authentic academic practice of sharing research findings with members of the community. In doing so, they were continuing to experience becoming as psychologists, historians, political scientists, geographers, economists, and sociologists. This environment had the effect of placing students in the midst of a transformative transition. More specifically, their participation in the practices of their disciplinary communities, and their reflection on these experiences, helped them begin to move from their roles as students to fuller participation in a disciplinary or professional community (Henscheid et al., 2019; Masiello & Skipper, 2013).

As this example highlights, high-impact practices such as undergraduate research, global learning, service learning, internships, and capstone experiences can be intentionally designed and delivered to support transitions. And at the foundation of this design process is attention to community, participation, and becoming.

Conclusion

This discussion of relationships, reflection, and risk underscores an essential, but often unarticulated objective of the work of supporting college students in transition: At its core, this work is about helping students experience connection.

We raised this issue somewhat casually in Chapter 4, but it is worth revisiting as we conclude this chapter. One aspect of college that can feel so troublesome to students is the disconnection that often results when they are navigating transitions. Indeed, transitions are frequently accompanied by feelings of unfamiliarity, separation, or marginalization. Consider, for example, the challenges of being a new transfer student on a campus. You are physically disconnected from the familiar place you just left; socially disconnected from the peers, faculty, and advisors from your previous institution; and if you have not yet declared a major or academic "home," the courses you are taking likely feel disconnected from your future, values, and goals. Whether they involve transferring to a new institution, arriving on campus as a first-generation student, searching for a major, or leaving college to venture into the workforce, transitions are marked by the "pain of disconnection" (Palmer, 1993, p. x.).

This pain is particularly pronounced when transitions are seen merely as movement, adjustment, or development toward some future state of comfortable stability. When transitions are defined in these ways, the disconnection students feel is likely to seem to them as nothing more than the inevitable and unproductive discomfort of being a newcomer or encountering some other element of unfamiliarity. To students, this disconnection feels like a barrier to comfort and serves no real purpose or function other than to signal to us that we do not yet belong.

While supporting transitions does, fundamentally, involve helping students experience a sense of connection and wholeness, approaching transitions as a venue for becoming is grounded in a core set of assumptions relative to the issues of connection and disconnection. First, while supporting transitions is aimed at helping students experience reconnection and wholeness, there is no way to completely avoid the pain of disconnection during times of transition. Second, though uncomfortable, the pain of disconnection can, in certain circumstances, serve an educative function if it leads students to seek after or search for connection and meaning. And third, transition programming and initiatives should minimize some forms of disconnection (e.g., those characterized by institutional environments that marginalize, discriminate, isolate, or deny access to community, participation, and becoming) while leveraging the educative disconnection (Dewey, 1938/1997; Louis & Hulme, 2020) that opens the door for becoming. This educative disconnection can signal to students that they are positioned for learning while providing an element of productive discomfort and uncertainty that nudges them to establish new community ties, engage in growth-promoting participation, and, ultimately, experience becoming as they embrace new ways of being and participating with those in their institutional community.

So, as we head into Chapter 7 and shift to exploring the practical application of these ideas for institutional leaders, we hope you are seeing that supporting transitions is grounded in the modes of transition: community, participation, and becoming. We also hope you are seeing more clearly how interrelated those three concepts are and the way they work together to provide opportunities for transformative learning during times of transition. Finally, we hope our brief discussion of the role of relationships, reflection, and risk has set your mental wheels in motion and planted a few seeds for practical starting steps you can take to approach the work of supporting transitions in new and refined ways on your campus.

Crucial Considerations

The following questions can help guide or initiate conversations with key partners on your campus or in your research networks and serve as starting points for rethinking transition theory and/or implementing changes in practice:

- How are possible relationships for students in transition constructed and distributed across your campus? What opportunities exist for participation and becoming as a community experience?

- Further questions about the construction and distribution of relationships include:

  o How can students in transition be supported in developing relationships that both foster new connections and community, while also preserving students' important ties with communities outside of the institution?

  o Who has access to powerful relationships that support transitions? Who does not? How can classrooms, institutions, and policies be restructured to level the relational playing field for students?

- What forms of reflection are students most commonly engaged in? When in their experience does this reflection take place? Are some forms of reflection more powerful in facilitating becoming than others? How can we structure reflective experiences in ways that honor diverse ways of knowing?

- How could the concept of a risk audit inform practice on your campus? What new areas of research could be explored based on the concept of a risk audit? Possible questions for a risk audit could include:

  o What unnecessary or unproductive risks do students take during transitions on our campus? Are these risks disproportionately borne by marginalized and under-resourced groups?

  o To what degree do we share risk with students on our campus?

  o How can we more effectively support students, faculty, and others in recognizing and understanding the role of risk in learning and transitions?

  o Where do we see "exemplars" of productive risk-taking (among both students and faculty)? How can we effectively share these stories to shift culture and practice?

Chapter 7 | Implications for Institutional Leaders

In Chapter 1 we answered the question "Who is this book for?" by discussing several potential "audiences" for our ideas, including practitioners, program directors, and professors in higher education graduate programs. Collectively, we referred to these folks as "thought leaders" and made a plea to this community of readers to remember that it takes a village to support students in transition.

Before we end the book, we want to make sure to acknowledge another category of thought leader: institutional leaders. Whether you're a vice president, provost, dean, or in some other senior-level post, you have a responsibility to support transitions at the institutional level. If you thumbed straight to this chapter looking for ideas and recommendations specific to your work, we hope you will also spend some time with the preceding chapters to give yourself more context and a broader perspective of the new theory–practice paradigm we have introduced throughout.

To help you hit the ground running, here is an executive summary of our foundational arguments so far:

- Supporting transitions is more than just helping students move into a new phase of college or adjust to new environments or programs. *Transitions are opportunities for transformation and becoming.*

- The field of higher education needs to expand people's thinking about what it means to support students in transitions beyond a short list of episodic, time-bound punctuations such as the first year, second year, or senior year. Instead, we

> need to acknowledge that college is composed of a protracted series of transitions that flow into, out of, and through one another.

- Supporting students in transition doesn't just mean "orienting" them to what's new. It's about *offering them belonging in communities on campus* by providing the chance to *participate with faculty and peers* in the experiences advertised in TV spots and glossy brochures and highlighted on campus tours.

With all institutional leaders have on their plate, some might wonder why any of this talk of supporting transitions matters. It is a fair question. Although nearly any institutional leader reading this chapter will have a department, a committee, or at best a "team of one" who has been charged with leading campus efforts to support students in transition (e.g., the orientation folks, enrollment management, or unit responsible for the first-year experience), this chapter still holds value for the leaders who oversee the work of these individuals and teams. We hope to convince leaders that paying attention to the way their institution thinks about and supports transition will affect other things they are accountable for, including diversity and inclusion; engagement in high-impact practices; academic progression; and the closure of institutional equity gaps. We will connect the dots between those critical issues and transitions as we get further into the chapter. But we will conclude this intro by discussing another issue that is almost certainly on campus leaders' radar: belonging.

Certainly, college campuses have always wanted students to feel welcome and connected enough to stay and graduate. However, the recent focus on students' sense of belonging is part of a broader change in thinking that is taking hold. For decades, colleges have pointed the finger at student deficits to explain many problems, including low retention rates, student disengagement, and failure to develop skills and abilities critical for careers and civic engagement. However, there is a growing recognition and acceptance that, first, institutions bear a moral and ethical responsibility to deliver on the explicit and implicit promises made upon admission to students about their capability to succeed on campus (e.g., Braxton et al., 2004; Hartman & Young, 2021; Mayhew et al., 2016; McNair et al., 2022; Nunn, 2021; Schreiner et al., 2020a). And second, helping students deepen their sense of belonging is one of the most effective ways to help them achieve traditional measures of college success (Strayhorn, 2012). In fact, a focus on belonging has been described as not just something nice to do, but as a "strategic question" central to institutional survival (Lu, 2023). So, the stakes are high.

Transitions present a key opportunity to both deepen student learning and cultivate feelings of belonging. However, as we have argued throughout the book, traditional thinking and practice related to transitions have not been as helpful as we all would have hoped—particularly for students in underrepresented or marginalized identity groups, whose numbers grow with every new admissions class.

In this chapter, we return to the three modes of transition—community, participation, and becoming—to highlight key implications that institutional leaders should consider as they explore ways they can be part of the campus-wide work of supporting students in transition.

Communicating a New Vision of the Goals and Purposes of Transition Work

While we hope the ideas shared in this book will have something of a grassroots impact and influence the thinking and practice of faculty, academic advisors, and program directors on your campus, individual efforts, though noble, likely will not be enough. Like nearly any paradigmatic or cultural shift, the journey from viewing *transitions as movement or adjustment to transitions as becoming* will require leaders willing to do the hard work of setting a new vision grounded in this (re)thinking about transitions. The changes we have argued for throughout this volume will only be impactful inasmuch as they are paired with leaders' efforts to proactively provide a new vision to help those they lead to reframe how they think about the work of supporting transitions. While the power of support, encouragement, and vision in the institutional change process might seem obvious, we mention it here because one of your most essential roles as an institutional leader is to offer vision and strategic direction for your campus.

This strategic focus is particularly critical in today's higher education landscape, in which we all face growing skepticism about the value of a college education. No doubt due in large part to the disruptions associated with COVID-19, college enrollment in the United States has dropped for six consecutive semesters from spring 2020 to fall 2022 (National Student Clearinghouse Research Center, 2023). Even for those students who plowed through the pandemic or who have returned to campus, there is unmistakable evidence they are finding their experience far less engaging and relevant than they would like. In the recent *State of the Student 2022* report produced by Wiley academic publishing (Wiley, 2023), more than half of the undergraduate students surveyed reported feeling disengaged and uninterested in their classes. When asked what sorts of adjustments would help address these issues, students overwhelmingly asked for "current, relevant content that's applicable to the real world and promotes interaction" as well as "company-based projects, simulations, scenarios, and connections with real professionals in the field" (Wiley, 2023, p. 6).

Ultimately, students are looking for learning experiences and environments that move beyond mere acquisition and understanding of decontextualized course content, to a college experience that (a) offers them entrée to what they often refer to as "real-life" communities outside the classroom and institution, and (b) allows them to apply their learning by participating in the real practices of these communities. Therefore, contextualized learning is also relational learning because contexts are communities of practice.

While on the surface, these challenges might appear to have little to do with college transitions and be more about higher education's failure to provide students with contextualized learning opportunities, one of our primary arguments is that the work of supporting transitions is, at its core, about precisely that issue. If what students want is an experience that is more relevant, applicable, interactive, and relational, the modes of community, participation, and becoming introduced in the preceding chapters offer paths forward for supporting transitions as well as providing students with a more contextualized learning experience.

As we did throughout our discussion of *theory–practice* in Chapter 5, we encourage you to consider several key questions that can help to guide this re-envisioning process; evaluate the extent that you and your colleagues are currently using the modes of community and participation to foster becoming; and begin to find potential sites of innovation and aspects of the student journey in which to focus your redesign efforts:

- What disciplinary, civic, and professional communities do your students have access to?

- What partnerships could be brokered to expand this network of communities?

- When in the student journey are students on your campus first provided opportunities to connect with these various extramural communities?

- How can you offer these connections earlier in students' experience?

- Do the programs and curricula on your campus provide students with the knowledge and skill to participate in these communities (albeit as newcomers and novices)?

- Do coursework and assessments encourage participation in these communities?

- How are you and other institutional leaders being explicit about approaching transitions as becoming?

Again, the work of supporting students in transition by offering access to communities and meaningful opportunities for participation is the work of the entire campus, so this isn't all on you as a leader. However, you do play a key role in helping your colleagues rethink and reframe the way they see transitions. Our hope is that you can lead others to embrace the opportunities they have to not just help students move into, move through, or adjust to the various aspects of their college experience, but rather to help them experience transformation and becoming during those transitions.

Identifying Invisible Sites of Marginalization in Transitions

In Chapters 1 and 5, we claimed that any conversation about transition is inherently about access, equity, and inclusion. We then discussed in Chapter 5 the importance of de-neutralizing transitions by building equity-minded (McNair et al., 2020) and race-conscious (Harper, 2009) practices into our efforts to support students in transition. This chapter is a natural place to continue that conversation and discuss the implications of our theoretical position for institutional leaders. Those of you in these roles can supplement the heroic efforts of your colleagues in classroom, advising, and co-curricular spaces by working to root out systemic inequities and widespread practices that serve as barriers to the transformation and becoming that are possible during transitions, particularly for historically underrepresented, underserved, and excluded student populations.

At this juncture, it is worth acknowledging the complexity of such equity-minded work in today's political climate. While institutional leaders might be willing to work toward closing equity gaps, in some cases (particularly for public, state-funded institutions) legislative actions may hamper institutions' ability to engage in this work in explicit ways. Institutions in these situations will surely face potential political and financial repercussions from focused efforts to support racially marginalized communities under the current controversy over initiatives and programs labeled "diversity, equity, and inclusion."

However, one of the reasons we feel so strongly about the need to rethink the way we support students in transition is that doing so can provide a somewhat stealthy way of addressing equity gaps, in that transitions impact all students on a college campus. Thus, a focus on improving transition experiences does not, on the surface, target any particular group of students. Yet, as we will discuss, intentional efforts to improve how we support students in transition—particularly those transitions associated with equity gaps—is likely to have the greatest benefit for those students who we historically have failed to support in ethical ways.

This process of finding inequitable spaces of transition begins by disaggregating the data to uncover differential outcomes across various student subpopulations, including first-generation students, students of color, and low-income students. We acknowledge that this more equity-minded approach to data analysis and assessment has happened much more often on college campuses in recent years. However, most of this work has focused on a narrow set of standard student success outcomes: retention, persistence, and graduation. Certainly, these common measures of student success offer insight into the experiences of students in transition. When institutional leaders become overly focused on these metrics, however, they are more likely to overlook several invisible transitions in the college experience that significantly affect institutional measures of success and, more importantly, the success and well-being of individual students.

An in-depth or comprehensive discussion of all the various forms of transition students experience is beyond the scope of this chapter. However, we will discuss a small number of these "invisible sites of marginalization" as examples of the spaces institutional leaders should consider when developing campus-wide efforts to better support college student transitions. These include gateway and foundational courses, developmental education, high-impact practices, and the experience of students on academic probation.

Before moving forward with our discussion of these spaces and accompanying recommendations for how to better support transitions in these contexts, we feel it important to note that what follows could very well have been placed in a chapter aimed specifically at faculty members. Another pair of authors might very well have chosen to structure the book in that way; however, we have intentionally directed this chapter to institutional leaders, as the comprehensive and systemic changes needed to better support transitions must ultimately be driven by those at the top.

Certainly, faculty members are essential stakeholders in the work of supporting students in transition (particularly in the areas we focus on in the remainder of this chapter). And the fact that no chapter in this book is devoted exclusively to faculty members is by no means meant to minimize their role in shaping students' experiences. Faculty bear the responsibility to do all they can in their classrooms, labs, and lecture halls to eliminate equity gaps. Further, we hope faculty members reading this book will find ways to use the modes of transition we have introduced as conceptual tools for refining how they support students.

However, we strongly believe that faculty members' ability to do things such as improve gateway courses and engage students in high-impact practices is, at least in part, dependent on the conditions in which they do their work. Institutional leaders are the primary architects of the macro-level systems, environments, and settings in which teaching and learning ultimately take place. In this chapter, we have chosen to write primarily to those institutional leaders. Nevertheless, we hope that both leaders and faculty realize the importance of seeing this work as a shared responsibility and one that requires close collaboration.

Gateway and Foundational Courses

In a workshop at the 2017 American Historical Association, David Pace, the historian and scholar of teaching and learning, remarked that up until quite recently, "the classroom was like the bathroom. You knew something important happened there, and you *never* talked about it!" (Pace, 2017). Though Pace was referring to the irony of not attending to what happens in the classroom as it relates to broad efforts to support student success, we find a similar gap in the thinking and practice around the classroom's role in college transitions. While learning communities, orientation programs, first-year seminars, sophomore-year programs, and other traditional transition initiatives are valuable, they tend to have a relatively minimal impact on the most fundamental element of the student experience: the classroom.

What's more, a particular type of class has been shown to have an outsized impact on students in transition. You likely know this type of class well—it is usually taken during the first or second year of college; tends to be taught in a large lecture hall with hundreds of students; prioritizes "coverage" of content; and might be known to students on your campus as a "killer" or "weed out" course (often in a STEM discipline). Over the past few years, these courses have come to be known formally as *gateway* or *foundational courses*. Efforts to close equity gaps and improve the experiences of students in transition must include attention to the experiences of students in these gateway courses. And institutional leaders, more than anyone else on campus, have the moral responsibility, institutional authority, and resource capital necessary to lead these critical reform efforts.

Again, efforts to improve the experiences of students in transition hold tremendous implications for issues of access and equity. For example, we know that students with minoritized identities in STEM fields who receive low grades or are forced to repeat gateway courses are at significantly higher risk of abandoning their goals for STEM careers and switching to non-STEM fields (e.g., Rask, 2010; Weston et al., 2019). Studies of gateway course outcomes have also shown that students on the margins who are otherwise in good academic standing, but who earn a D, F, W, or I grade in a gateway course are at elevated risk of not even returning to their institution for the next year (Koch & Drake, 2018).

But these trends only become clear when institutional leaders are willing to pull back the curtain and look at course-level data for foundational gateway classes, then disaggregate the data to shed light on the experiences of student sub-populations. When they do, it becomes evident that students who have trying experiences in gateway courses are disproportionately from underrepresented student groups (Koch, 2017a; Koch, 2017b).

Consequently, we call on institutional leaders to undertake wide-scale efforts to refine and improve the teaching, learning, and assessment in the foundational gateway courses on their campus. But we are not simply calling on you to engage in this work. We offer the three modes of transition—community, participation, and becoming—as a theory–practice lens to help you and your colleagues consider how you can tackle this daunting challenge. In fact, as we have considered the biggest critiques of gateway courses (i.e., rote learning in large classes with no real peer or instructor interaction; abstract concepts disconnected from meaningful contexts; excessive focus on acquisition and content "coverage"), the modes of transition seem to offer a potent antidote for aspects of gateway courses that systematically disadvantage the most vulnerable students on your campus.

As we have done throughout this book, we will leave it to you and your colleagues to consider what community, participation, and becoming mean for the students and gateway courses on your campus. But we do offer a few recommendations for starting down this path:

- *Democratize the data and share it with deans, department chairs, and instructors of gateway courses.* We deeply believe that most faculty members, at their core, care about the experiences and success of the students in their classroom. However, most do not understand how the way they teach and assess in their large courses systematically disadvantages particular segments of the student population. Providing access to key data on student performance, particularly when the data is disaggregated to show trends across various demographic groups, is the first step to helping faculty make necessary refinements. While some faculty might embark on this path on their own, in most cases, senior-level leaders will need to lead a systematic approach.

- *Give support and guidance in making sense of the data.* Particularly outside of STEM fields, faculty members might need (and greatly appreciate) helpful and kind support in making sense of complicated data sets. We are not suggesting dumbing down this information, but highlighting the data reports or dashboards for faculty through some sort of workshop or seminar, led by folks from the office of assessment, will likely be much more helpful than emailing a report and leaving the faculty to go it alone. Again, this might seem like the responsibility of faculty members (and at some level it is), but institutional leaders have the responsibility to encourage these efforts, remove barriers preventing faculty from engaging in this work, and make institutional resources available for training, workshops, etc.

- *Approach faculty in a spirit of collaboration and goodwill.* No one likes to hear that the way they are doing their work is harming students. Further, we do not believe any faculty are intentionally trying to marginalize students in their classroom. But the fact is, improvements need to be made. Efforts to help faculty improve what goes on in their classroom will often be met with resistance or defensiveness. However, if institutional leaders can make clear that the goal is to offer support and resources for making curricular and pedagogical improvements (rather than to punish and publicly shame), two things are much more likely to happen. First, gateway course experiences will improve. Second, word will get out that you are acting in goodwill, and you can start to build a coalition of colleges and departments willing to engage in the arduous work of curricular reform. Another way to put this might be to avoid punishing those who are willing to shine a light on their practices. Instead, celebrate, recognize, and reward genuine efforts to improve gateway courses.

- *Finally, engage faculty leaders and gateway instructors in dialogue around the three modes of transition.* We hope you will introduce faculty to the ideas in this book and find ways to engage key stakeholders in structured dialogue to help incorporate community, participation, and becoming into gateway courses, even in small ways. This could happen in reading groups or seminars, or through quality enhancement plans or other formal institutional improvement efforts.

Developmental Education

Another frequently overlooked classroom space with tremendous implications for transitions is the domain of developmental education. As is the case for low grades in gateway courses, students placed into developmental education coursework tend to be disproportionately first-generation, low-income, enrolled part time, and from historically underrepresented populations (Roberts, 2023). These patterns have important implications for transitions because enrollment in developmental education courses is associated with both increased student cost and time to graduation.

Certainly, the stated goals of developmental education are to be celebrated; we all want the students who enter our institutions to be poised for success and to possess the foundational knowledge and skill to move forward to graduation. However, placement into developmental education can send a subtle but pernicious message to students that they do not belong and that institutions do not see them as capable of success. For students from privileged backgrounds who come into college with an inherent confidence and sense of belonging, this messaging can be easy to brush off. They might think, "I know what I'm doing; these people are idiots." But for students who came to college with any degree of *belonging uncertainty* (Walton & Cohen, 2007), being told they are not yet ready to take "real classes" can lead them to erroneously believe they might never be ready to be successful in college.

In Chapter 5, we introduced the *self-directed placement* approach to developmental education at the Community College of Baltimore County (CCBC). It is an excellent example of how the invisible transitions associated with developmental education can be thoughtfully structured to engage students as *legitimate peripheral participants* (Lave & Wenger, 1991). These transitions can also position students for both belonging and becoming during a vulnerable period, as they are determining whether they can really claim membership in their new community.

As a leader on your campus, you might consider several other aspects of developmental education as a space for transition:

- *Begin by asking important questions about who is enrolled in developmental education and what happens to them once they finish their developmental education coursework.*

Are students with minoritized identities overrepresented in developmental education courses on your campus? How might policies related to developmental education or current advising practices be contributing to this trend? What percentage of students who enroll in developmental education persist and graduate? What do these data look like when disaggregated?

- *Consider how community, participation, and becoming might inform the way you and your colleagues structure developmental education.* Again, CCBC serves as a helpful model. The college's self-directed placement approach attends to community by enrolling students in both a traditional introductory English course and a paired support course, avoiding the marginalization and disconnection that result when a student is placed into a non-credit bearing course not asked of any other students on campus. Additionally, students are invited to be active participants in course registration, as they are provided both the information and personal support necessary to decide for themselves which of two types of first-year English course structures will best meet their needs (i.e., either the traditional English 101 course or an English 101 course paired with a support course). When academic advisors offer students real partnership in course placement decisions, they strongly communicate that (a) all students admitted to the institution are seen as valued members of the campus community, and (b) the institution honors and values the lived experiences and individualized ways of knowing that students bring with them to campus. Finally, this self-directed approach to developmental education course placement signals to students that they are becoming full participants in the academic community at CCBC.

- *Design developmental education experiences grounded in relationships, reflection, and educative risk* (see Chapter 6 for more on these ideas and their connection to the modes of transition). Relationships with peers, faculty, and academic advisors are vitally important for students enrolled in developmental education, as they tie students to the broader institutional community and become a powerful source of belonging and support. Also, as CCBC illustrates, these relationships should begin during the advising and placement process. They can then become an important vehicle for engaging students in reflection on the course structure(s) to best support their transition into the institution, the support or resources that will be most helpful, and how their early classroom experiences are preparing them for future coursework. Finally, while providing students with agency in making decisions about course placement might seem risky, we hope you and your colleagues will see this as productive and educative risk that leverages the power of community, participation, and becoming for students enrolled in developmental education coursework.

As discussed in Chapter 6, attending to these elements of the transition experience opens the door for transformative learning opportunities and rich relational and community-based connections. It is a key aspect of attending to equity, inclusion, and belonging for a population of students often overlooked in discussions of college transitions.

High-Impact Practices

As we have suggested throughout this book, high-impact practices (HIPs) stand as a powerful example of the type of experiences that can facilitate becoming during times of transition. Whether it is a study abroad experience, undergraduate research, an internship, or a culminating capstone course, HIPs leverage many of the key characteristics of powerful transition experiences—community, participation, relationships, reflection, and risk—to create learning environments where students are well-positioned for becoming. Consequently, there is plentiful evidence connecting engagement in HIPs with a host of positive outcomes for students. Students who report having participated in HIPs are more likely to be engaged in deep learning (Finley & McNair, 2013), demonstrate higher GPAs (Vogelgesang & Astin, 2000), and be more comfortable working collaboratively in groups (Lopatto, 2010). Additionally, HIPs participation is associated with higher retention rates (O'Donnell et al., 2015), better job opportunities after graduation (Miller et al., 2018), and a higher likelihood of admission to graduate school (Barlow & Villarejo, 2004; Greenman et al., 2022).

Further, HIPs offer particularly powerful promise in closing institutional equity gaps between historically underserved student populations and their more privileged peers (Finley & McNair, 2013; Huber, 2010; Greenman et al., 2022; O'Donnell et al., 2015). However, the very students who benefit the most from HIPs (i.e., first-generation students, transfer students, students of color, and low-income students) are the least likely to have access to and participate in these transformative experiences (Kuh et al., 2017; NSSE, 2018). Thus, this is one area of the student transition experience ripe for examination by institutional leaders.

Building on our call for a more equity-minded approach to transitions in Chapter 5, we invite campus leaders to examine the landscape of HIPs on their campus through an equity framework; readers might consider the work of Garces and Gordon da Cruz (2017), Hatch (2020), or McNair et al. (2020). Viewing the role of HIPs in transitions through this critical lens raises key questions, including:

- How do traditional ways of defining HIPs create a class of experience inaccessible to broad swaths of our students because of factors such as cost, available time, and access to traditional in-person learning experiences?

- How do the academic reward systems in place for faculty on your campus either discourage or incentivize faculty investment in engaging in HIPs with students and embedding HIPs within course curricula?

- How can student academic records systems be redesigned so that engagement in HIPs is visible and measurable?

Using these questions as guides, you and your colleagues can begin to explore ways to make engagement in HIPs more equitable and more likely to offer opportunities for becoming during times of transition among a wider range of students. Again, the very best solutions will be those you and your team develop based on the context and characteristics of your campus. We offer just a few suggestions to get you started:

- *Expand your thinking about what "counts" as a HIP beyond the formal list of 11 practices suggested by Kuh (2008).* High-impact practices can take a variety of forms, depending on student characteristics, institutional context, available resources, and other factors (Kuh, 2008; Kuh & O'Donnell, 2013). We actually find the list of eight key elements of HIPs (see Kuh & O'Donnell, 2013 or Kuh et al., 2017 for an in-depth discussion of these) to be an invaluable guide when considering how to design educational experiences with high impact, even if these eight elements do not yet appear on the list of 11 "official" HIPs.

- *Consider how traditional HIPs could be modified and adapted to provide access to a wider range of students.* As previously mentioned, understanding the key characteristics of HIPs provides a set of design principles that can be applied to any number of student experiences. For example, shortened study abroad experiences that maintain an immersive feel and provide meaningful engagement with diverse cultures can serve as an alternative to traditional semester-long experiences. Similarly, institutions might explore how virtual learning communities for first-year students could be designed to provide opportunities for both community and participation in authentic practices associated with the broader academic community (Greenman et al., 2022).

- *Explore how faculty reward structures could be modified to recognize the time, commitment, skill, and expertise required of faculty members to include HIPs in their work.* There is a "cost" to faculty members who take the time to engage in HIPs with students outside of the classroom or who do the hard pedagogical design work to incorporate HIPs into their curricula. As committed to student learning as faculty members might be, taking the time to integrate HIPs in their work means taking time away from another activity the institution formally recognizes as worthy of reward and recognition. As a leader, you can leverage your institutional capital to provide resources to support faculty development focused on HIPs, financial incentives to drive innovation, and budget monies to fund student participation in HIPs (Kezar & Holcombe, 2017).

- *Make participation in HIPs a core and central aspect of the experience of every student who enrolls on your campus.* Kuh et al. (2017) might have said it best: "We need a higher education infrastructure better than the one we inherited, one in which HIPs are *built into the college experience for all who enroll* [emphasis added], rather than a supplement or innovation on the margins" (p. 13). We wholeheartedly agree. If we know engagement in HIPs improves outcomes, particularly for our most vulnerable students, we bear a moral and ethical responsibility to work to ensure that participation in HIPs is not just another in a long list of educational luxuries afforded to the already privileged. Yes, HIPs bring a costlier upfront sticker price than the traditional three credit-hour large lecture we have come to seemingly worship. However, as has been argued elsewhere, if we were to shift the way we evaluate cost-effectiveness—from measuring enrollments to measuring completions—HIPs could prove to be more cost effective in the long run because more students who participate in them will persist to graduation (Kuh et al., 2017; MDRC, 2015; Metro Academies, 2013; Wellman, 2010).

- *Find ways to make student participation in HIPs more visible on student transcripts and academic records.* Just as faculty reward systems influence decisions around faculty time, students make assumptions about what the institution values based on what is recognized and counted on their academic record. Maybe even more importantly, modified academic record systems that document student participation in HIPs will allow you and your colleagues to move beyond simplistic reliance on student self-reported data and provide more accurate understanding of the "state of HIPs" on your campus.

Academic Probation

Academic probation, though often seen as a phenomenon that occurs because of some other "failed" transition, has been described as a transition in its own right—specifically, "a transition between unsatisfactory performance to either acceptable academic standing or to dismissal" (Arcand & Leblanc, 2011, p. 3). Though certainly disruptive and often painful for students, the transitions associated with academic probation can, under particular conditions, become "profound teachable moments and critical junctures in the educational process" (Keup, 2022, p. ix). But this depends heavily on how institutions frame these transitions and offer support and guidance to students at these times of heightened vulnerability. Following our review of conceptualizations of transition in

Chapter 2, the descriptions of academic probation we have just presented frame the transitions in academic probation, and perhaps the rationale behind the status itself, as movement, adjustment, and development. Notwithstanding, being placed on academic probation can trigger critical reflection on the part of students and open the door for the sorts of transformational learning (Suchan, 2016) associated with the other transitions discussed in this book.

Moreover, in parallel with nearly every other significant transition we have highlighted, the academic probation experience disproportionately impacts students on the margins, including students of color (Hamman, 2018; Mathies et al., 2006; Nance, 2007; Tovar & Simon, 2006), low income, and first-generation college students (Young & Weigel, 2022). Consequently, attending to the transition experiences of students on academic probation has clear implications for broader efforts to close equity gaps and further institutional priorities relative to diversity, equity, and inclusion. Additionally, there are real financial costs for institutions when students on academic probation leave campus and never return, resulting in lost tuition revenue and penalties related to performance-based funding. But most importantly, when we admit a student to one of our campuses, we have a moral and ethical responsibility to deliver on the implicit promise we made in their congratulatory admissions letter, namely, that we believe they can succeed and we will do our part to help them realize that success.

So, how can we reimagine the possibilities for academic probation as transformative transition-as-becoming?

As Morris and Harris (2022) argue, when it comes to academic probation, institutional leaders and policymakers are engaged in the work of *choice architecture* (Thaler & Sunstein, 2009), in that they are positioned to craft the environments where students experience academic probation and the options available to them during these critical times of transition. Supporting students on academic probation is more than just neutral administrative work. Indeed, "designing [academic recovery] processes could elevate this practice from rote administrative action to transformational learning" (Morris & Harris, 2022, p. 29). So the natural question is how?

As a preface to the recommendations that follow, we acknowledge that supporting students on academic probation, as with any transition, is complex and multifaceted. Thus, the ideas we share here are not meant in any way to serve as a reductionist, over-simplified "how-to" guide, magically transforming the experiences of students affected by academic probation. However, by examining academic probation policies and practices through the lens of the modes of transition, campuses can identify a host of solutions and innovations that, together, support students whose experience of becoming during college includes the process of academic probation. Institutional leaders can better support students on academic probation by attending to the following:

- *Increase the scope of recovery and support efforts by developing a suite of varied interventions designed to offer support to students experiencing academic probation* (e.g., a course; an online module; ongoing mentoring or support from a peer leader, faculty member or academic advisor), then allowing students agency in determining the most helpful intervention for them. Passive, voluntary programs leave the onus for successful transitions largely on the student and represent an abdication of responsibility on the institution's part.

- *Offer relational support, community, and belonging by maintaining regular contact and ongoing connection with students during academic probation.* This is particularly important when students are taking required time away from campus as part of academic suspension or academic dismissal. Without consistent outreach and support during these times, students have little choice but to assume the institution never really cared whether they were part of the community to begin with.

- *Evaluate and refine the language used in academic probation notification letters.* For a moment, consider what it must be like for a student to read this in a letter: "Due to your recent academic performance, you have been placed on Academic Suspension beginning with the fall semester. As part of Academic Suspension, you will be required to take a minimum of 12 months away from the institution. For more information about the policies related to Academic Suspension, click here." How much of a sense of community do you think you would feel? How likely would you want to try to come back in a year? How confident would you feel that returning was even possible? And how supported would you feel? In contrast with more traditional approaches, psychologically attuned language can avoid academic probation being viewed as punitive and marginalizing, and instead help students feel support, hope, and direction, despite the natural negative emotions that come with these notifications. *Psychologically attuned messaging* (a) frames probation or suspension as a process of learning and growth, rather than a label; (b) acknowledges the varied reasons why a student might find themselves on academic probation; (c) normalizes the experience of academic difficulty by communicating that it is a common experience for students; and (d) offers both hope and support for returning to good academic standing or returning to the institution (see Brady, 2017; Brady et al., 2019; and Waltenbury et al., 2018 for more on the concept of *psychologically attuned notification letters*). Not only does this type of language signal that the institution still values the student as a member of the community, it also subtly implies the transition, though undesirable in many ways, is an opportunity for becoming.

- Leverage the power of relationships by *offering students on academic probation connection to a specific person at the institution.* This individual can serve as a navigator, guide, mentor, and support during the entirety of the probation or dismissal process. Ideally, they would contact the student soon after notification of a change in academic standing, follow up regularly, and provide personalized support as the student navigates the transition back into good academic standing. Additionally, in a way like the *self-directed placement* process at the Community College of Baltimore County, this advisor, coach, or faculty member could intentionally find ways to invite the student to participate more fully in the recovery process by engaging them in regular reflection on their experience. This reflection could explore the factors that led to academic challenges, resources that would be most important to access during the recovery process, meaningful activities to participate in during time away, or a timeline for return that will best serve the student given their unique circumstances. Moreover, low-cost remote meeting technology makes this sort of engagement and interaction possible whether a student remains proximate to the physical campus while they are on probation or not.

Ultimately, when institutional leaders approach academic probation as a critical transition and then thoughtfully consider how the three modes of transition might inform institutional policy and practice, these transitions can foster learning and becoming. Indeed, Suchan (2016) found that students on academic probation can experience "healing," closure, and meaningful learning and growth during these times. This is particularly true when students are placed in relationship with supportive institutional actors who then invite students to reflect on and articulate what they are learning through their experiences. Students can also relate how these experiences impact their personal learning and career goals, and what kinds of support they need to advance toward these goals.

Conclusion

As a leader on your campus, you play a critical role in supporting transitions and helping both students and colleagues see these times as opportunities for becoming. We hope this chapter has provided new conceptual insights related to the nature of transitions, raised questions you can use to spark important dialogue on your campus, and brought attention to overlooked transitions or aspects of the student experience that require more work. While this short chapter might not have given you enough for a detailed strategic plan or fully formed course of action, we hope it has provided a place to start. We also hope you are now thinking of at least a few ways in which community, participation, and becoming can be leveraged more strategically to support your students.

As discussed earlier in this chapter, faculty members will be essential partners in your efforts to reconceptualize how your institution supports students in transition. While it truly does take a village to support students in this position, any attempt to support transitions that does not emphasize the need to improve the experiences of students in instructional spaces will fall short. We call on institutional leaders to use the ideas set forward in this book to initiate campus-wide conversations that explore how faculty members, advisors, student success professionals and others can work collaboratively to support students in transition more effectively.

These conversations will be particularly important on smaller campuses, where folks often wear multiple hats and have limited resources to draw from. We fully acknowledge that there are costs (financial and otherwise) associated with most, if not all of the recommendations made in this book. So while community, participation, and becoming might look very different on the campus of a small, private, liberal arts college compared with a community college or a large public university, we believe these ideas have relevance regardless of the specific features of your institution.

For example, a small institution might not have the resources required to offer large numbers of students the chance to engage in undergraduate research, thereby helping them become full participants in the campus community. But that institution's relatively small numbers might allow for a new-student orientation experience that features small, enriching, faculty or peer leader-led discussions of a common summer reading text. Such an experience is one relatively low-cost, yet relationship-rich way of inviting students to participate and contribute to the institution's intellectual work. The key for institutional leaders is creating spaces where colleagues can reflect on and explore together the implications of these ideas for their particular challenges, constraints, opportunities, and available resources. We invite you to consider the communities on your campus (or beyond) that you can engage with to explore, debate, and design transition experiences that open doors for your students to become the type of people you promised they could be when you admitted them. Like you, we really do believe those promises.

Crucial Considerations

- What additional "invisible" sites of marginality not addressed in this chapter might be present on your campus? How might you go about convening diverse groups of stakeholders across campus to both identify and address these sites of marginalization?

- What institutional challenges could be addressed through focused attention to supporting transitions in the ways this book describes?

- How might technology be leveraged to develop cost-effective and flexible ways of supporting students in transition? How could technology enhance efforts to offer community and participation to students? When might technology serve as a barrier to community and participation?

- How might faculty be invited as key partners in efforts to more effectively support transitions? What barriers might currently exist that keep faculty from helping students experience community, participation, and becoming in the ways described in this book?

- The invisible sites of marginality discussed in this chapter could create opportunities for colleagues across campus to collaborate on what these areas might be. Individuals in different roles often have different lived experiences that would help to minimize these invisible sites. What are the mechanisms to convene various people from across campus to discuss these issues?

PART 4:
CHARTING A PATH FORWARD

Chapter 8 | Past, Present, and Future of Rethinking Transition Theory: Reflection, Integration, New Directions

This book is a snapshot in time.

Well, here we are: the final chapter of this book on rethinking college student transition theory. In Chapter 1, we talked about our journey that led us to this work and how it brought us a sense of *optimistic longing*. Now that we are at the end of the writing process, we still feel that sense of optimism and longing, but it has changed because we have changed. As St. Pierre (2015) points out:

> *Writing allows us to think things we might not have thought by thinking alone. Writing takes us places we might not have gone if we had not written. We must think in order to write the next word, the next sentence, the next theory. An idea simply thought may seem brilliant until it is written. A brilliant unthought idea may appear as we write. Writing forces us to textualize the rigorous confusion of our thinking (p. 5305).*

As such, writing is an important process of doing, thinking, and becoming. What's more, writing a book is a process of learning that has elements of community and participation, as well. We see our work as an opportunity to engage with the community of higher education scholar-practitioners, to offer a forum to participate with our colleagues, and to be part of an ongoing process of becoming. It is in this spirit of community, participation, and becoming that we offer this book as both an invitation to participate in the rethinking with us and a request to join you in your own reimagining of student transitions.

Therefore, what we have written is not a final word on any individual matter we have discussed. Rather, it is a retracing of where we have been, a "you are here" marker on a map, and a point of departure, all at once. It is a rear-view mirror through which we can see what we have passed, what is following us, and what we might look like wearing a new set of lenses, all while looking forward at the road ahead.

What Has Passed

In Chapter 2, we presented a review and critique of previously and long-held conceptualizations of transitions. Building on and expanding previous works that outlined and categorized definitions and theories of transitions (e.g., Colley, 2007; Gale & Parker, 2014; Quinn, 2010), we presented descriptions of transitions imagined as movement, adjustment, development, or sociocultural processes. Key to the argument we are forwarding throughout this book is that these previously held notions of student transitions fall short of describing the transitions' fullness and complexity.

We want to make our position clear, however: of course, all these things happen. Movement happens in transition, requiring adjustment. Psychosocial and cognitive development happen during transitions. And our ideas of becoming and situated learning are an example of transitions as a sociocultural process. With all the risks (and resulting questions about the origins) of using a cliché, there is no need to throw the baby out with the bathwater. We simply and strongly suggest that these previous theoretical positions offer a limited and limiting view of student transitions for all the reasons outlined in Chapter 2.

We also find that our review of the history of transition theory brings with it a position to consider important questions for our collective future rethinking of student transitions. For instance, what are the socio-emotional aspects of entering a new community as a novice in a position on the periphery? What are the emotions that the climate of the community and access to opportunities for participation evoke in students as they move into these spaces?

Clearly, students will have to navigate unexpected and unfamiliar environments and circumstances whenever they are newcomers. Moreover, institutions and their agents (e.g., faculty, student affairs professionals, administrators) must understand issues of power in order to create co-agentic spaces where students can participate and find belonging. We imagine research and descriptions of theory–practice that tell these stories and expand on what socio-emotional community, participation, and becoming might look like.

One practical concern we must contend with is the tradition—particularly in student affairs scholarship, professional preparation, and practices—of the use of student development theory to understand student learning and, resultantly, transition. Conceptualizations of becoming are much more open to the flux, movements, situations, and paradoxes that students experience than are present in a developmental approach to understand transitions. To briefly revisit: Images of transition as development are frequently cast as linear, progressive from one stage to the next, and represent movement from one relatively stable state to the next. Where regression occurs, it is the psychological revisiting of a previous state, not developmental reversion.

Contemporary and emergent research on student transitions, however, shows the process of transition is not always so neat as the developmental perspective suggests. One pragmatic example of this concern is that research and assessment processes frequently frame learning outcomes as movement of students along a developmental trajectory. Such trajectories could include developing purpose, establishing identity through a major or career decision, taking a leave of absence, or being placed on academic probation (see Chickering & Reisser, 1993; Dial, 2022; Hartman & Young, 2021; Keup, 2019; Schlossberg et al., 1989; Young, 2016; Young et al., 2017). Assessment under the developmental perspective would measure student progression along the stages and cast student regression as either a failure of the program, the measurement, or the students. Alternately, becomingist perspectives would encourage us to understand those findings from a more nuanced and student-oriented perspective. Sure, such findings might represent an issue that merits response, but they might also represent overall student growth in agency and internalized authorship. Higher education needs more thinking, examples, and literature that help us reconcile and contemplate well-tested theories of development alongside understandings of becoming.

Another series of questions that prior conceptualizations of transitions as a sociocultural process suggest are: How do social constructions of identity (e.g., race, gender, ability) interact with new identities as a member of an academic community? How can transition as becoming create opportunities for an expansive view of education rather than a restrictive one? In response, we call for increased attention to research on how reimagined perspectives on transition can help educators better deliver on higher education's promise to expand opportunities for students to become members of multiple communities, without having to give up their connection to communities that matter to them.

We also acknowledge that many of the suggestions we point to throughout the book involve faculty. To be clear, we have seen manifold examples of faculty members who believe strongly in mentorship, creating positive and authentic rapport with students, and cultivating the kinds of relationships we have signaled as important contributors to transition through community, participation, and becoming. We both also sit in the multifaceted world of "faculty." Because we currently occupy different professional roles and orientations within that category, we recognize the different forces that shape faculty behavior and decisions that we and our colleagues make.

We envision future work tackling the tensions and organizational realities that create conditions for faculty to engage in the relationships and provide opportunities for authentic participation in the ways critical for supporting student transitions. This work includes understanding institutional reward structures, messaging from academic leadership, and support from centers for teaching and learning in promoting faculty's key role in supporting student transitions across the totality of the student experience. We also need to tackle questions that tease out the nuances between the ways faculty establish processes of socialization and how they foster legitimate peripheral participation in academic and other college communities of practice. We envision research that helps understand the ways they are similar and the things that make LPP powerful and set apart from socialization practices.

Now, we return to how we are rethinking transitions. Chapter 2 presented a definition of transitions as a progressing dynamic activity system. As part of this system, students are agentic actors who have meaningful connections with other agentic actors, who then have formal and more experienced roles in a collection of communities that comprise an institution. Chapter 3 expanded on these ideas to describe how student transition represents becoming members of an academic community through an ongoing process that includes:

- strengthening meaningful connections with others in the community;

- ongoing authentic participation in the practices of the community, leading to increased awareness of and experience with knowledge, skills, tools, and language that facilitate further participation; and

- opening up a trajectory of ways of being, doing, and thinking that are congruent with student goals and images of self.

Our Present View

Throughout the book, we have built on our current conceptual and operational definitions of transition to point to and focus on the importance of the modes of community, participation, and becoming (as outlined in Chapter 4). As expressed earlier in this chapter, the writing of this book itself has had elements of community, participation, and becoming. These three modes are also useful in framing where we presently sit with our (re)thinking of transitions.

We are both proud and engaged members of several communities of practice in higher education. These include our departments, institutions, professional organizations, academic associations, networks of peers, and the classrooms and educational spaces where we get to participate alongside our students. While tackling this work, we continually have talked about how we can further engage with our communities to continue our (re)thinking of transition theory. One thing we continue to grapple with is the question: What does the community of those who are working with the theory–practice of transition see as the places where this theory specifies practice and where practice specifies the theory? We continue to look for ways to involve members of our communities in our own process of becoming better thinkers, whether through discussions after a presentation, requesting feedback on drafts, or asking questions of those we encounter with intriguing new perspectives.

If you are reading this, we hope you will accept an invitation to join us in a community of practice. We want to hear your thoughts about transitions and how these ideas show up for you in your work. We also want to hear about things we have missed, glossed over, or distorted. Sending this invitation naturally poses risks; we might be exposed for not being as clever as we thought, and our email inboxes might be filled with constant critiques of this work.

Then again, what is community without relationship and participation?

We have had several conversations about finding ways to participate with colleagues in the revision and refining of these perspectives. Naturally, the best place for us to start is within our own spheres of influence. We have considered how we can participate with stakeholders, such as students, staff, faculty, administrators, and policymakers, in rethinking the student transitions situated on our campuses. This could include setting up meetings with transition-focused colleagues across campus to hear from them and share our ideas.

Along the same lines, we have worked on finding ways to participate with our students in the theory–practice on our campuses. This has shown up in how we have shaped our pedagogical practices to expand the opportunities for students to participate in transition programs we have the pleasure to work with. But participation requires a mutuality, a co-agentic position, so we have crafted ways to bring the students in our communities into the conversation as members of research teams on the topic, through informal conversations about these ideas, or as contributing participants in research. As we have begun this process, we have found ourselves in a position to develop relationships, reflect on the meaning of the work, and involve the students in the risk inherent in the work of research (see Chapter 6 for a more in-depth discussion of relationships, reflection, and risk).

Finally, our present view requires us to ask what it means for a theory to *be* while also in a position of *becoming*? Writing down our ideas fixes them in time and runs the risk of concretizing them. Yet, as authors and readers, our thinking on any topic is rarely, if ever, fixed in time. So we have to accept the limitations that come with the benefits of writing as thinking and becoming. As authors, we want to communicate that we are constantly attending to temporal matters such as what comes next, what has preceded our thinking that we missed and that should be incorporated, and what needs to be reconsidered and expanded. We are serious about our commitment to these ideas and will continue to think, research, and write on transitions. As with any process of becoming, this will happen in fits and starts, changes in formats and expressions, and even that which might look like steps backward. We want you to help us find ways to sustain a vision of transition that is in flux and is open and responsive to ever-present changes to situations, people, and society.

What Lies Ahead

If this whole process of rethinking student transitions is also one of becoming, you might be asking yourself, "What's next?" Hopefully Chapters 6 and 7 provided you with some useful, practical guidance on how to apply the theory–practice we have outlined in the book. Before we finish, we offer a few more recommendations on what to do next.

We both have had the pleasure of working on a research team on the topic of transition theory with a bright doctoral student from the University of Georgia named Aaron. While talking with Dallin recently, Aaron shared his frustration about books on theory like ours:

"When you're a student, you can learn about a theory, what it says, what it's all about, what it means … and then that's it. There is no explanation of what to do with it. How to 'use it'—how to apply it, what it means for practice, what it looks like in real life."

Aaron, you make a very good point, likely one shared by many other graduate students, practitioners, administrators, and professors in higher education professional preparation programs, among all the others who encounter theories like this one. Hopefully we have provided good guidance on how to use the theory in Chapters 5, 6, and 7 as well as in this current chapter. Nevertheless, we think Aaron's observation serves as a valuable reminder that we should provide some final advice to readers on what to "do" with the theory. So here is what we would suggest you *do* with the ideas contained in this book.

Do:

- Experiment with ideas of community, participation, and becoming as you design and implement programs supporting students in transition.

- Use this theory as a mirror to examine your current philosophies and conceptualizations on students in transition.

- Accept our challenges to examine issues of power and agency; use this as a framework to understand how to create co-agentic definitions of success.

- Engage transition-as-becoming paired with situated learning as theoretical or conceptual frameworks in research.

- Experiment, test, refine, and revise our offered definition of transitions.

- Start dialogues with key stakeholders on your campus, in the professional associations you belong to, and with others who are among your professional communities.

- Consider this an invitation to participate in our community of practice; we sincerely want to move these ideas forward.

- Engage with us. Tell us what you think. Tell us what we've missed. Tell us what you think this points to that we have not considered. Tell us how this works or doesn't.

We also want to offer some perspectives on what we would ask readers not to do. So here is our list of *don'ts*.

Don't:

- Reduce the ideas we presented to justify concepts of transitions rooted in transition as movement, adjustment, development, or even simple sociocultural notions.

- See community, participation, or becoming as discrete aims in and of themselves or decontextualized apart from our definition of transition.

- Forget that students are your most important collaborators and stakeholders in any of this work.

- Stop believin'.

Final Thoughts

Why a rethinking and reimagining of college student transitions? We hope we have provided not only a compelling rationale for why we need to reconsider transitions, but also a compelling new way of thinking about them and an explanation of its importance for theory–practice. Whether you read the book chapter by chapter from cover to cover, or you have taken a more zig-zag approach, we hope you have found these ideas intriguing or useful. We hope that as you go forward and revisit these ideas, you will pay closer attention to the ways you think about how your students in transition encounter communities on campus, the access they have to authentic and progressively meaningful forms of participation with more experienced members of the community, and how these contribute to their becoming in ways aligned with their visions of self. We also hope this discussion leads to new forms of dialogue and opportunities to debate the meaning of the perspectives we have outlined. This is true whether they occur in your program meetings, with vice presidents or other similarly titled administrators, at academic conferences, or even over dinner at ACPA's Annual Convention the next time it takes place in Columbus, Ohio.

REFERENCES

American Association of Colleges and Universities (2020). *What liberal education looks like: What it is, who it's for, and where it happens*. American Association of Colleges and Universities.

Ames, M. E., Wintre, M. G., Pancer, S. M., Pratt, M. W., Birnie-Lefcovitch, S., Polivy, J., & Adams, G. R. (2014). Rural compared to urban home community settings as predictors of first-year students' adjustment to university. *Journal of College Student Development, 55*(2), 208–215. https://doi.org/10.1353/csd.2014.0016

An, B. P., & Taylor, J. L. (2019). A review of empirical studies on dual enrollment: Assessing educational outcomes. In M. B. Paulsen and L. W. Perna (Eds.), *Higher education: Handbook of theory and research* (Vol. 34, pp. 99–151). Springer.

Andrews, B. D. (2018). Delayed enrollment and student involvement: Linkages to college degree attainment. *The Journal of Higher Education, 89*(3), 368–396.

Anzaldúa, G. (2015). *Light in the dark/Luz en lo oscuro: Rewriting identity, spirituality, reality*. Duke University Press.

Arcand, I., & Leblanc, R. (2011). Academic probation and companioning: Three perspectives on experience and support. *Mevlana Intenational Journal of Education, 1*(2), 1–14.

Argyris, C., & Schön, D. (1996). *Organizational learning II: Theory, method, and practice.* Addison-Wesley.

Astin, A. W. (1977). *Four critical years: Effects of college on beliefs, attitudes, and knowledge.* Jossey-Bass.

Astin, A. W. (1984). Student involvement: A developmental theory for higher education. *Journal of College Student Personnel, 25*(4), 297–308.

Astin, A. W. (1993). *What matters in college? Four critical years revisited.* Jossey-Bass.

Attinasi, L. C. (1989). Getting in: Mexican Americans' perceptions of university attendance and the implications for freshman year persistence. *The Journal of Higher Education, 60*(3), 247–277.

Bailey, T. R., Hughes, K. L., & Karp, M. M. (2002). What role can dual enrollment programs play in easing the transition between high school and postsecondary education. *Journal for Vocational Special Needs Education, 24,* 18–29.

Baker, D. J., Arroyo, A. T., Braxton, J. M., & Gasman, M. (2020). Understanding student persistence in commuter historically black colleges and universities. *Journal of College Student Development, 61*(1), 34–50.

Baker, R. W., & Siryk, B. (1999). *SACQ: Student Adaptation to College Questionnaire Manual.* Western Psychological Services.

Baker, S., & Irwin, E. (2019). Disrupting the dominance of 'linear pathways': How institutional assumptions create 'stuck places' for refugee students' transitions into higher education. *Research Papers in Education, 36*(1), 75–95.

Baldwin, A., Bunting, B. D., Daugherty, D., Lewis, L., & Steenbergh, T. (2020). *Promoting belonging, growth mindset, and resilience to foster student success.* University of South Carolina, National Resource Center for The First-Year Experience & Students in Transition.

Barefoot, B. O., Gardner, J. N., Cutright, M., Morris, L. V., Schroeder, C. C., Schwartz, S. W., Siegel, M. J., & Swing, R. L. (2005). *Achieving and sustaining institutional excellence for the first year of college.* Jossey-Bass.

Barefoot, B. O., Griffin, B. Q., & Koch, A. K. (2012). *Enhancing student success and retention throughout undergraduate education: A national survey.* The John N. Gardner Institute for Excellence in Undergraduate Education.

Barlow, A. E., & Villarejo, M. (2004). Making a difference for minorities: Evaluation of an educational enrichment program. *Journal of Research in Science Teaching, 41*(9), 861–881.

Barnett, R. (2009). Knowing and becoming in the higher education curriculum. *Studies in Higher Education, 34*(4), 429–440.

Barry, M. (2005). *Youth policy and social inclusion.* Routledge.

Bassett, B. S. (2020). Better positioned to teach the rules than to change them: University actors in two low-income, first-generation student support programs. *The Journal of Higher Education, 91*(3), 353–377.

Baxter Magolda, M. B. (2004). Learning partnerships model. In M. B. Baxter Magolda & P. M. King (Eds.), *Learning partnerships: Theory and models of practice to educate for self-authorship* (pp. 37–62). Stylus.

Baxter Magolda, M. B. (2009). *Authoring your life: Developing your internal voice to navigate life's challenges.* Stylus.

Baxter Magolda, M. B. (2014). Self-authorship. *New Directions for Higher Education, 2014*(166), 25–33.

Bean, J. P., & Metzner, B. S. (1985). A conceptual model of nontraditional undergraduate student attrition. *Review of Educational Research, 55*(4), 485–540.

Becker, M. A. S., Schelbe, L., Romano, K., & Spinelli, C. (2017). Promoting first-generation college students' mental well-being: Student perceptions of an academic enrichment program. *Journal of College Student Development, 58*(8), 1166–1183.

Bensimon, E. M. (2018). Reclaiming racial justice in equity. *Change: The Magazine of Higher Learning, 50*(3-4), 95–98.

Berger, J. B., & Milem, J. F. (1999). The role of student involvement and perceptions of integration in a causal model of student persistence. *Research in Higher Education, 40*(6), 641–664.

Bess, J. L., & Dee, J. R. (2008). *Understanding college and university organization: Theories for effective policy and practice: Volume II—dynamics of the system.* Stylus.

Bowman, N. A., Jarratt, L., Jang, N., & Bono, T. J. (2019). The unfolding of student adjustment during the first semester of college. *Research in Higher Education, 60*, 273–292.

Brady, S. T. (2017). *A scarlet letter? Institutional messages about academic probation can, but need not, elicit shame and stigma* [Doctoral dissertation, Stanford University]. ProQuest Dissertations Publishing.

Brady, S., Fricker, T., Redmond, N., & Gallo, M. (2019). *Academic probation: Evaluating the impact of academic standing notification letters on the experience and retention of students* (Follow-up report). Higher Education Quality Council of Ontario.

Braxton, J. M., Hirschy, A. S., & McClendon, S. A. (2004). *Toward understanding and reducing college student departure.* (ASHE-ERIC Higher Education Report Series, Vol. 30, No. 3). Jossey-Bass.

Bridges, W. (2004). *Transitions: Making sense of life's changes.* Da Capo.

Bronfenbrenner, U. (1979). *The ecology of human development: Experiments by nature and design.* Harvard University Press.

Brown, J. S., & Duguid, P. (1991). Organizational learning and communities-of-practice: Toward a unified view of working, learning, and innovation. *Organization Science, 2*(1), 40–57.

Bunting, B. D., & Williams, D. D. (2017). Stories of transformation: Using personal narrative to explore transformative experience among undergraduate peer mentors. *Mentoring and Tutoring, 25*(2), 166–184.

Caffarella, R. S., & Merriam, S. B. (1999). Perspectives on adult learning: Framing our research. In A. Rose (Ed.), *Proceedings of the 40th Annual Adult Education Research Conference.* LEPS Press.

Carpenter, D. M., Kaka, S. J., Tygret, J. A., & Cathcart, K. (2018). Testing the efficacy of a scholarship program for single parent, post-freshmen, full time undergraduates. *Research in Higher Education, 59*(1), 108–131.

Carter, D. F., Locks, A. M., & Winkle-Wagner, R. (2013). From when and where I enter: Theoretical and empirical considerations of minority students' transition to college. In M. B. Paulsen (Ed.), *Higher education: Handbook of theory and research* (Vol. 28, pp. 93–149). Springer.

Chambliss, D. F., & Takacs, C. G. (2014). *How college works.* Harvard.

Chickering, A. W., & Reisser, L. (1993). *Education and identity.* Jossey-Bass.

Clouder, L., Karakus, M., Cinotti, A., Ferreyra, M. V., Fierros, G. A., & Rojo, P. (2020). Neurodiversity in higher education: A narrative synthesis. *Higher Education, 80*(4), 757–778.

Coertjens, L., Brahm, T., Trautwein, C., & Lindblom-Ylänne, S. (2017). Students' transition into higher education from an international perspective. *Higher Education, 73*(3), 357–369.

Cohen, G. L. (2022). *Belonging: The science of creating connection and bridging divides.* W. W. Norton & Company.

Cole, D., Newman, C. B., & Hypolite, L. I. (2020). Sense of belonging and mattering among two cohorts of first-year students participating in a comprehensive college transition program. *American Behavioral Scientist, 64*(3), 276–297.

Colley, H. (2007). Understanding time in learning transitions through the lifecourse. *International Studies in Sociology of Education, 17*(4), 427–443.

Collier, P. J. (2015). *Developing effective student peer mentoring programs: A practitioner's guide to program design, delivery, evaluation, and training.* Stylus.

Complete College America. (2012). *Remediation: Higher education's bridge to nowhere.* Indianapolis, IN: Author. https://completecollege.org/wp-content/uploads/2017/11/CCA-Remediation-final.pdf

Covarrubias, R., Jones, J., & Johnson, R. (2020). Exploring the links between parent–student conversations about college, academic self-concepts, and grades for first-generation college students. *Journal of College Student Retention: Research, Theory & Practice, 22*(3), 464–480.

Cox, B. E., Nachman, B. R., Thompson, K., Dawson, S., Edelstein, J. A., & Breeden, C. (2020). An exploration of actionable insights regarding college students with autism: A review of the literature. *The Review of Higher Education, 43*(4), 935–966.

Cox, B. E., Thompson, K., Anderson, A. M., Mintz, A., Locks, T., Morgan, L., Edelstein, J., & Wolz, A. (2017). College experiences for students with autism spectrum disorder: Personal identity, public disclosure, and institutional support. *Journal of College Student Development, 58*(1), 71–87.

Cuevas, S. (2020). Ley de la vida: Latina/o immigrant parents experience of their children's transition to higher education. *The Journal of Higher Education, 91*(4), 565–587.

Daddow, A. (2016). Curricula and pedagogic potentials when educating diverse students in higher education: Students' Funds of Knowledge as a bridge to disciplinary learning. *Teaching in Higher Education, 21*(7), 741–758.

Dahl, R. A. (1961). *Who governs? Power and democracy in an American city.* Yale University Press.

Deleuze, G., and Guattari, F. (1987). *A thousand plateaus: Capitalism and schizophrenia.* Continuum.

Dewey, J. (1933). *How we think.* Prometheus Books.

Dewey, J. (1938/1997). *Experience and education.* Simon & Schuster.

Dial, M. T. (Ed.) (2022). *Academic recovery: Supporting students on academic probation.* University of South Carolina, National Resource Center for The First-Year Experience & Students in Transition.

Duncheon, J. C., & Relles, S. R. (2020). "We're caught in between two systems": Exploring the complexity of dual credit implementation. *The Review of Higher Education, 43*(4), 989–1016.

Duran, A., Dahl, L. S., Stipeck, C., & Mayhew, M. J. (2020). A critical quantitative analysis of students' sense of belonging: Perspectives on race, generation status, and collegiate environments. *Journal of College Student Development, 61*(2), 133–153.

Durkheim, E. (1897). *Suicide.* (Trans. by J. A. Spaulding and G. Simpson). Free Press (1951).

Ecclestone, K. (2007). Resisting images of the 'diminished self': The implications of emotional well-being and emotional engagement in education policy. *Journal of Education Policy, 22*(4), 455–470.

Ecclestone, K., Biesta, G., & Hughes, M. (2010). Transitions in the lifecourse: The role of identity, agency and structure. In K. Ecclestone, G. Biesta, & M. Hughes (Eds.). *Transitions and learning through the lifecourse* (pp. 1–15). Routledge.

Emirbayer, M., & Mische, A. (1998). What is agency? *American Journal of Sociology, 103*(4), 962–1023.

Fairclough, N. (1992). *Discourse and social change.* Polity Press.

Felten, P., Gardner, J. N., Schroeder, C. C., Lambert, L. M., Barefoot, B. O., & Hrabowski, F. A. (2016). *The undergraduate experience: Focusing institutions on what matters most.* John Wiley & Sons.

Felten, P., & Lambert, L. M. (2020). *Relationship-rich education: How human connections drive success in college.* JHU Press.

Finley, A., & McNair, T. (2013). *Assessing underserved students' engagement in high-impact practices.* Association of American Colleges and Universities.

Fish, J., & Syed, M. (2018). Native Americans in higher education: An ecological systems perspective. *Journal of College Student Development, 59*(4), 387–403.

Flint, M. A., Kilgo, C. A., & Bennett, L. A. (2019). The right to space in higher education: Nonbinary and agender students' navigation of campus. *Journal of College Student Development, 60*(4), 437–454.

Fowler, M., & Luna, G. (2009). High school and college partnerships: Credit-based transition programs. *American Secondary Education, 38*(1), 62–76.

Franke, R., & Bicknell, B. (2019). Taking a break, or taking a class? Examining the effects of incentivized summer enrollment on student persistence. *Research in Higher Education, 60*, 606–635.

Gale, T., & Parker, S. (2014). Navigating change: A typology of student transition in higher education. *Studies in Higher Education, 39*(5), 734–753.

Garces, L. M., & Gordon da Cruz, C. (2017). A strategic racial equity framework. *Peabody Journal of Education, 92*(3), 322–342.

Gardner, J., & Van der Veer, G. (1998) *The senior year experience: Facilitating integration, reflection, closure, and transition.* Jossey-Bass.

Garrison-Wade, D. F., & Lehmann, J. P. (2009). A conceptual framework for understanding students' with disabilities transition to community college. *Community College Journal of Research and Practice, 33*(5), 415–443.

Giani, M. S. (2019). The correlates of credit loss: How demographics, pre-transfer academics, and institutions relate to the loss of credits for vertical transfer students. *Research in Higher Education, 60*(8), 1113–1141.

Goldberg, A. E., Kuvalanka, K. A., & Black, K. (2019). Trans students who leave college: An exploratory study of their experiences of gender minority stress. *Journal of College Student Development, 60*(4), 381–400.

Gorgorió, N., Planas, N., & Vilella, X. (2002). Immigrant children learning mathematics in mainstream schools. In G. de Abreu & N. C. Presmeg (Eds.), *Transitions between contexts of mathematical practices* (Mathematics Education Library, Vol. 27, pp. 23–52).

Gravett, K. (2021). Troubling transitions and celebrating becomings: From pathway to rhizome. *Studies in Higher Education, 46*(8), 1506–1517.

Greenman, S. J., Chepp, V., & Burton, S. (2022). High-impact educational practices: Leveling the playing field or perpetuating inequity? *Teaching in Higher Education, 27*(2), 267–279.

Griffin, K. A., & Gilbert, C. K. (2015). Better transitions for troops: An application of Schlossberg's transition framework to analyses of barriers and institutional support structures for student veterans. *The Journal of Higher Education, 86*(1), 71–97.

Griffin, K. A., & McIntosh, K. L. (2015). Finding a fit: Understanding Black immigrant students' engagement in campus activities. *Journal of College Student Development, 56*(3), 243–260.

Grosz, E. (1994). *Volatile bodies: Toward a corporeal feminism.* Indiana University Press.

Hallett, R. E., Kezar, A., Perez, R. J., & Kitchen, J. A. (2020). A typology of college transition and support programs: Situating a 2-year comprehensive college transition program within college access. *American Behavioral Scientist, 64*(3), 230–252.

Hamman, K. J. (2018). Factors that contribute to the likeliness of academic recovery. *Journal of College Student Retention: Research, Theory & Practice, 20*(2), 162–175.

Hamshire, C., & Jack, K. (2016). Becoming and being a student: A Heideggerian analysis of physiotherapy students' experiences. *The Qualitative Report, 21*(10), 1904–1919.

Hanson, C. (Ed.). (2014). In search of self: Exploring student identity development. *New Directions for Higher Education, 166*. John Wiley & Sons.

Harper, C. E., Zhu, H., & Marquez Kiyama, J. (2020). Parents and families of first-generation college students experience their own college transition. *The Journal of Higher Education, 91*(4), 540–564.

Harper, S. R. (2009). Race-conscious student engagement practices and the equitable distribution of enriching educational experiences. *Liberal Education, 95*(4), 38–45.

Hartman, C. (2023). A review of vertical and horizontal transfer student transitions and experiences. *Higher education: Handbook of theory and research, 38*, 1–57. Springer.

Hartman, C., Callahan, R., & Yu, H. (2021). Optimizing intent to transfer: Engagement and community college English learners. *Research in Higher Education, 62*(6), 789–828.

Hartman, C., & Young, D. G. (2021). *Sustaining support for sophomore students: Results from the 2019 National Survey of Sophomore-Year Initiatives*. University of South Carolina, National Resource Center for The First-Experience & Students in Transition.

Hatch, D. K., & Garcia, C. E. (2017). Academic advising and the persistence intentions of community college students in their first weeks in college. *The Review of Higher Education, 40*(3), 353–390.

Hatch, D. K., Mardock-Uman, N., Garcia, C. E., & Johnson, M. (2018). Best laid plans: How community college student success courses work. *Community College Review, 46*(2), 115–144.

Hatch, R. (2020, April 28). *New framework to infuse diversity, equity, and inclusion into faculty professional development*. The Report. Illinois State University. https://news.illinoisstate.edu/2020/04/new-framework-to-infuse-diversity-equity-and-inclusion-into-faculty-professional-development/

Heiser, C. A., Prince. K., & Levy, J. D. (2017). Examining critical theory as a framework to advance equity through student affairs assessment. *The Journal of Student Affairs Inquiry, 3*(1), 1–17.

Henning, G., & Lundquist, A. E. (2022). Using assessment to advance equity. *New Directions for Student Services, 2022*, 178–179, 185–194.

Henning, G. W., & Roberts, D. (2016). *Student affairs assessment: Theory to practice.* Stylus.

Henscheid, J. M. (2012). Senior seminars and capstones. In M. S. Hunter, J. R. Keup, J. Kinzie, & H. Maietta (Eds.), *The senior year: Culminating experiences and transitions* (pp. 91–109). University of South Carolina, National Resource Center for The First-Year Experience & Students in Transition.

Henscheid, J. M., Skipper, T. L., & Young, D. G. (2019). Reflection, integration, application: Intentional design strategies for senior capstone experiences. *New Directions for Higher Education, 2019*(188), 91–100.

Hersh, R., & Keeling, R. (2011). *We're losing our minds: Rethinking higher education.* Palgrave Macmillan.

Hills, J. (1965) Transfer shock: The academic performance of the transfer student. *The Journal of Experimental Education, 33*(3), (Spring, 1965).

Howitt, S. M., Wilson, A. N., & Higgins, D. M. (2022). Unlearning, uncovering and becoming: experiencing academic writing as part of undergraduate research. *Teaching in Higher Education,* 1–16.

Huber, B. J. (2010). *Does participation in multiple high impact practices affect student success at Cal State Northridge? Some preliminary insights.* California State University Northridge, Office of Institutional Research.

Hughes, A. N., & Gibbons, M. M. (2018). Understanding the career development of underprepared college students. *Journal of College Student Retention: Research, Theory & Practice, 19*(4), 452–469.

Hurtado, S., Alvarez, C. L., Guillermo-Wann, C., Cuellar, M., & Arellano, L. (2012). A model for diverse learning environments: The scholarship on creating and assessing conditions for student success. In J. C. Smart and M. B. Paulsen (Eds.), *Higher education: Handbook of theory and research* (Vol. 27, pp. 41–122). Springer.

Hurtado, S., & Carter, D. F. (1997). Effects of college transition and perceptions of the campus racial climate on Latino college students' sense of belonging. *Sociology of Education, 70*(4), 324–345.

Ibarra, H., & Petriglieri, J. L. (2010). Identity work and play. *Journal of Organizational Change Management, 23*(1), 10–25.

Iloh, C. (2018). Toward a new model of college "choice" for a twenty-first-century context. *Harvard Educational Review, 88*(2), 227–244.

Jabbar, H., Epstein, E., Sánchez, J., & Hartman, C. (2021). Thinking through transfer: Examining how community college students make transfer decisions. *Community College Review, 49*(1), 3–29.

Jenkins, D., Lahr, H., & Mazzariello, A. (2021). *How to achieve more equitable community college student outcomes: Lessons from six years of CCRC research on guided pathways.* Community College Research Center, Teachers College, Columbia University. https://files.eric.ed.gov/fulltext/ED615154.pdf

Johnson, S. R., & Stage, F. K. (2018). Academic engagement and student success: Do high-impact practices mean higher graduation rates? *The Journal of Higher Education, 89*(5), 753–781.

Jury, M., Smeding, A., Stephens, N. M., Nelson, J. E., Aelenei, C., & Darnon, C. (2017). The experience of low-SES students in higher education: Psychological barriers to success and interventions to reduce social-class inequality. *Journal of Social Issues, 73*(1), 23–41.

Kamer, J. A., & Ishitani, T. T. (2021). First-year, nontraditional student retention at four-year institutions: How predictors of attrition vary across time. *Journal of College Student Retention: Research, Theory & Practice, 23*(3), 560–579.

Kaufman, P. (2014). The sociology of college students' identity formation. *New Directions for Higher Education, 2014*(166), 35–42.

Keeling, R.P. (Ed.). (2004). *Learning reconsidered: A campus-wide focus on the student experience.* National Association for Student Personnel Administrators & American College Personnel Association.

Keeling, R. P., Underhile, R., & Wall, A. F. (2007). Horizontal and vertical structures: The dynamics of organization in higher education. *Liberal Education, 93*(4), 22–31.

Keup, J. R. (2019). Institutional attention to and integration of the first-year experience. In D. G. Young (Ed.), *2017 National Survey on the First-Year Experience: Structures for supporting student success* (Research Reports on College Transitions No. 9, pp. 19–32). University of South Carolina, National Resource Center for The First-Year Experience & Students in Transition.

Keup, J. R. (2022). Foreword. In M. T. Dial (Ed.), *Academic recovery: Supporting students on academic probation.* University of South Carolina, National Resource Center for The First-Year Experience & Students in Transition.

Keup, J. R., & Petschauer, J. W. (2011). *The first-year seminar: Designing, implementing, and assessing courses to support student learning and success. Volume One: Designing and administering the course.* University of South Carolina, National Resource Center for The First-Year Experience and Students in Transition.

Kezar, A., & Holcombe, E. (2017). Support for high-impact practices: A new tool for administrators. *Liberal Education, 103*(1), n1.

Kezar, A., & Kitchen, J. A. (2020). Supporting first-generation, low-income, and underrepresented students' transitions to college through comprehensive and integrated programs. *American Behavioral Scientist, 64*(3), 223–229.

Kezar, A., & Maxey, D. (2014). Faculty matter: So why doesn't everyone think so? *Thought & Action, 2014*, 29–44.

Kim, Y. K., & Sax, L. J. (2017). The impact of college students' interactions with faculty: A review of general and conditional effects. In M. B. Paulsen (Ed.), *Higher education: Handbook of theory and research* (Vol. 32, pp 85–139). Springer.

Kincheloe, J. L. (2011). Describing the bricolage. In K. Hayes, S. R. Steinberg, & K. Tobin (Eds.), *Key works in critical pedagogy*. Sense Publishers.

Kitchen, J. A., Hallett, R. E., Perez, R. J., & Rivera, G. J. (2019). Advancing the use of ecological systems theory in college student research: The ecological systems interview tool. *Journal of College Student Development, 60*(4), 381–400.

Koch, A. K. (2017a). Many thousands failed: A wakeup call to history educators. *Perspectives on History, 55*(5), 18–19.

Koch, A. K. (2017b). It's about the gateway courses: Defining and contextualizing the issue. *New Directions for Higher Education, 2017*(180), 11–17.

Koch, A. K., & Drake, B. M. (2018). *Digging into the disciplines I: Accounting for failure—The impact of principles of accounting courses on student success and equitable outcomes.* https://static1.squarespace.com/static/59b0c486d2b857fc86d09aee/ t / 5 d 9 4 e 2 e 7 c 9 f a 3 2 0 4 4 3 b 7 7 5 f 2 / 1 5 7 0 0 3 8 5 0 5 7 2 9 / Digging+Into+the+Disciplines+Accounting+for+Failure+022619.pdf

Koo, K., Baker, I., & Yoon, J. (2021). The first year of acculturation: A longitudinal study on acculturative stress and adjustment among first-year international college students. *Journal of International Students, 11*(2), 278–298.

Kopp, J. P., & Shaw, E. J. (2016). How final is leaving college while in academic jeopardy? Examining the utility of differentiating college leavers by academic standing. *Journal of College Student Retention: Research, Theory & Practice, 18*(1), 2–30.

Kuh, G. D. (2008). *High-impact educational practices: What they are, who has access to them, and why they matter.* Association of American Colleges and Universities.

Kuh, G. D., Cruce, T. M., Shoup, R., Kinzie, J., & Gonyea, R. M. (2008). Unmasking the effects of student engagement on first-year college grades and persistence. *The Journal of Higher Education, 79*(5), 540–563.

Kuh, G. D., Kinzie, J., Buckley, J. A., Bridges, B. K., & Hayek, J. C. (2007). Major theoretical perspectives on student success in college. *Piecing together the student success puzzle: Research, propositions, and recommendations: ASHE Higher Education Report, 32*(5), 13–20.

Kuh, G. D., & O'Donnell, K. (2013). Ensuring quality and taking high-impact practices to scale. *Peer Review, 15*(2), 32–33.

Kuh, G., O'Donnell, K., & Schneider, C. G. (2017). HIPs at ten. *Change: The Magazine of Higher Learning, 49*(5), 8–16.

Kyndt, E., Donche, V., Trigwell, K., & Lindblom-Ylänne, S. (2017). *Higher education transitions: Theory and research.* Routledge.

Laanan, F. S. (2001). Transfer student adjustment. *New Directions for Community Colleges, 2001*(114), 5–13.

Laanan, F. S. (2004). Studying transfer students: Part I: Instrument design and implications. *Community College Journal of Research and Practice, 28*(4), 331–351.

Laanan, F. S., Starobin, S. S., & Eggleston, L. E. (2010). Adjustment of community college students at a four-year university: Role and relevance of transfer student capital for student retention. *Journal of College Student Retention: Research, Theory & Practice, 12*(2), 175–209.

Lane, S. R. (2020). Addressing the stressful first year in college: Could peer mentoring be a critical strategy? *Journal of College Student Retention: Research, Theory & Practice, 22*(3), 481–496.

Lave, J., & Wenger, E. (1991). *Situated learning: Legitimate peripheral participation.* Cambridge University Press.

Li, A. Y., & Ortagus, J. C. (2019). Raising the stakes: Impacts of the Complete College Tennessee Act on underserved student enrollment and sub-baccalaureate credentials. *The Review of Higher Education, 43*(1), 295–333.

Light, R. J. (2001). *Making the most of college: Students speak their minds.* Harvard University Press.

Lim, J. H., Interiano, C. G., Nowell, C. E., Tkacik, P. T., & Dahlberg, J. L. (2018). Invisible cultural barriers: Contrasting perspectives on student veterans' transition. *Journal of College Student Development, 59*(3), 291–308.

Linley, J. L. (2017). We are (not) all Bulldogs: Minoritized peer socialization agents' meaning-making about collegiate contexts. *Journal of College Student Development, 58*(5), 643–656.

Liou, D. D., Antrop-González, R., & Cooper, R. (2009). Unveiling the promise of community cultural wealth to sustaining Latina/o students' college-going information networks. *Educational Studies, 45*(6), 534–555.

Little, T. L., & Mitchell Jr., D. (2018). A qualitative analysis of undocumented Latino college students' movement towards developing purpose. *The Review of Higher Education, 42*(1), 137–172.

Lopatto, D. (2010). Undergraduate research as a high-impact student experience. *Peer Review, 12*(2), 27–31.

Louis, M. C., & Hulme, E. (2020). Thriving in the senior-year transition. In L. A. Schreiner, M. C. Louis, & D. D. Nelson (Eds.), *Thriving in transitions: A research-based approach to college student success* (2nd ed.) (pp. 171–191). University of South Carolina, National Resource Center for The First-Year Experience & Students in Transition.

Lu, A. (2023, February 14). Everyone is talking about 'belonging,' but what does it really mean? *The Chronicle of Higher Education, 69*(12). Retrieved March 10, 2023, from https://www.chronicle.com/article/everyone-is-talking-about-belonging

Lundberg, C. A. (2010). Institutional commitment to diversity, college involvement, and faculty relationships as predictors of learning for students of color. *The Journal of the Professoriate, 3*(2), 50–74.

Markus, H., & Nurius, P. (1986). Possible selves. *American Psychologist, 41*(9), 954.

Masiello, L., & Skipper, T. L. (2013). *Writing in the senior capstone: Theory and practice.* National Resource Center for The First-Year Experience and Students in Transition, University of South Carolina.

Mathies, C., Gardner, D., & Bauer, K. W. (2006). *Retention and graduation: An examination of students who earn academic probation* [Paper presentation]. SAIR Forum, Arlington, VA, United States.

Mayhew, M. J., Rockenbach, A. N., Bowman, N. A., Seifert, T. A., Wolniak, G. C., Pascarella, E. T., & Terenzini, P. T. (2016). *How college affects students: 21st century evidence that higher education works.* Jossey-Bass.

McCormick, A. C., Kinzie, J., & Gonyea, R. M. (2013). Student engagement: Bridging research and practice to improve the quality of undergraduate education. *In Higher education: Handbook of theory and research* (Vol. 28, pp. 47–92). Dordrecht: Springer Netherlands.

McDonough, P. M. (1997). *Choosing colleges: How social class and schools structure opportunity.* State University of New York.

McEwen, M. K. (2003). The nature and use of theory. In S. R. Komives & D. B. Woodard, Jr. (Eds.), *Student services: A handbook for the profession* (4th ed., pp. 153–178). Jossey-Bass.

McHenry-Sorber, E., & Swisher, K. (2020). Negotiating place and gender: Appalachian women's postsecondary transition experiences. *The Review of Higher Education, 43*(4), 1193–1226.

McNair, T. B., Albertine, S., Cooper, M. A., McDonald, N., & Major, T., Jr. (2016). *Becoming a student-ready college: A new culture of leadership for student success.* Jossey-Bass.

McNair, T. B., Albertine, S., McDonald, N., Major Jr., T., & Cooper, M. A. (2022). *Becoming a student-ready college: A new culture of leadership for student success* (2nd ed.). John Wiley & Sons.

McNair, T. B., Bensimon, E. M., & Malcom-Piqueux, L. (2020). *From equity talk to equity walk: Expanding practitioner knowledge for racial justice in higher education.* John Wiley & Sons.

McQueen-Ruark, R., & Schaller, M. A., (2022, October 1). *Taking a developmental and strategic approach to the second year* [Preconference workshop session]. 2022 National Conference on Students in Transition, Atlanta, GA, United States.

MDRC (2015). *Frequently asked questions about CUNY's Accelerated Study in Associate Programs* (ASAP). https://www.mdrc.org/publication/frequently-asked-questions-about-cuny-s-accelerated-study-associate-programs-asap

Means, D. R., Clayton, A. B., Conzelmann, J. G., Baynes, P., & Umbach, P. D. (2016). Bounded aspirations: Rural, African American high school students and college access. *The Review of Higher Education, 39*(4), 543–569.

Means, D. R., & Pyne, K. B. (2017). Finding my way: Perceptions of institutional support and belonging in low-income, first-generation, first-year college students. *Journal of College Student Development, 58*(6), 907–924.

Melendez, M. C. (2015). Adjustment to college in an urban commuter setting: The impact of gender, race/ethnicity, and athletic participation. *Journal of College Student Retention: Research, Theory & Practice, 18*(1).

Messer, K., Gallagher, J., & Hart, E. (2022). A path to equity, agency, and access: Self-directed placement at the community college of Baltimore County. In J. Nastal, M. Poe, & C. Toth (Eds.), *Writing placement in two-year colleges: The pursuit of equity in postsecondary education.* The WAC Clearinghouse; University Press of Colorado, pp. 85–105. https://doi.org/10.37514/pra-b.2022.1565.2.03

Metro Academies Initiative (2013). *Metro Academies lowers cost per graduate at a university and a community college.* https://rpgroup.org/Portals/0/Documents/PolicyMakers/CostStudy.pdf

Mettler, J., Carsley, D., Joly, M., & Heath, N. L. (2019). Dispositional mindfulness and adjustment to university. *Journal of College Student Retention: Research, Theory & Practice, 21*(1), 38–52.

Miles, S. (2000). *Youth lifestyles in a changing world.* Buckingham: Open University Press.

Miller, A. L., Rocconi, L. M., & Dumford, A. D. (2018). Focus on the finish line: Does high-impact practice participation influence career plans and early job attainment? *Higher Education, 75,* 489–506.

Miller, R. A. (2017). "My voice is definitely strongest in online communities": Students using social media for queer and disability identity-making. *Journal of College Student Development, 58*(4), 509–525.

Mintz, S. (2019, December 5). Reimagining college's third year. *Inside Higher Ed.* https://www.insidehighered.com/blogs/higher-ed-gamma/reimagining-college%E2%80%99s-third-year

Mokher, C. G., & Leeds, D. M. (2018). Can a college readiness intervention impact longer-term college success? Evidence from Florida's statewide initiative. *The Journal of Higher Education.* Advance online publication. https://doi.org/10.1080/00221546.2018.1525986

Moll, L. C., Amanti, C., Neff, D., & Gonzalez, N. (1992). Funds of knowledge for teaching: Using a qualitative approach to connect homes and classrooms. *Theory Into Practice, 31*(2), 132–141.

Morris, C., & Harris, A. (2022). Institutional policies on probation, dismissal, and reinstatement. In M. T. Dial (Ed.). *Academic recovery: Supporting students on academic probation.* University of South Carolina, National Resource Center for The First-Year Experience & Students in Transition.

Morton, J. M. (2019). *Moving up without losing your way: The ethical costs of upward mobility.* Princeton University Press.

Murdock-Perriera, L. A., Boucher, K. L., Carter, E. R., & Murphy, M. C. (2019). Places of belonging: Person- and place-focused interventions to support belonging in college. *In Higher education: Handbook of theory and research* (Vol. 34, pp. 291-323). Springer.

Museus, S. D., Yi, V., & Saelua, N. (2017). The impact of culturally engaging campus environments on sense of belonging. *The Review of Higher Education, 40*(2), 187–215.

Musoba, G. D., Jones, V. A., & Nicholas, T. (2018). From open door to limited access: Transfer students and the challenges of choosing a major. *Journal of College Student Development, 59*(6), 716–733.

Nance, M. (2007). The psychological impact of academic probation. *Diverse Issues in Higher Education, 24*(19), 12.

National Resource Center for The First-Year Experience & Students in Transition. (n.d.). *About us.* https://sc.edu/about/offices_and_divisions/national_resource_center/about/index.php

National Student Clearinghouse Research Center (2022, June). *Persistence and retention: Fall 2020 beginning postsecondary student cohort.* https://nscresearchcenter.org/wp-content/uploads/PersistenceRetention2022.pdf

National Student Clearinghouse Research Center (2023, February). *Current term enrollment estimates: Fall 2022 expanded edition.* https://public.tableau.com/app/profile/researchcenter/viz/CTEE_Fall2022_Report/CTEEFalldashboard

National Survey of Student Engagement (NSSE) (2018). *Engagement insights: Survey findings on the quality of undergraduate education. Annual results 2018.* Indiana University Center for Postsecondary Research.

Nelson, D. D., Vetter, D., & Vetter, M. K. (2020). Thriving from the start: Equipping students for success in the first year. In L. A. Schreiner, M. C. Louis, & D. D. Nelson (Eds.), *Thriving in transitions: A research-based approach to college student success* (2nd ed., pp. 53–77). University of South Carolina, National Resource Center for The First-Year Experience & Students in Transition.

Nicholson, N., & West, M. (1995). Transitions, work histories, and careers. In M. B. Arthur, D. T. Hall, & B. S. Lawrence (Eds.), *Handbook of career theory* (pp. 181–201). Cambridge University Press.

Niehaus, E. (2017). Building momentum in student engagement: Alternative breaks and students' social justice and diversity orientation. *Journal of College Student Development, 58*(1), 53–70.

Nora, A. (2004). The role of habitus and cultural capital in choosing a college, transitioning from high school to higher education, and persisting in college among minority and nonminority students. *Journal of Hispanic Higher Education, 3*(2), 180–208.

Nuñez, A. M., & Sansone, V. A. (2016). Earning and learning: Exploring the meaning of work in the experiences of first-generation Latino college students. *The Review of Higher Education, 40*(1), 91–116.

Nunn, L. (2021). *College belonging: How first-year and first-generation students navigate campus life*. Rutgers University Press.

O'Donnell, K., Botelho, J., Brown, J., González, G. M., & Head, W. (2015). Undergraduate research and its impact on student success for underrepresented students. *New Directions for Higher Education, 2015*(169), 27–38.

O'Donnell, V. L., Kean, M., and Stevens, G. (2016). *Student transitions in higher education: Concepts, theories and practices*. Higher Education Academy. https://s3.eu-west-2. amazonaws.com/assets.creode.advancehe-document-manager/documents/hea/ private/resources/student_transition_in_higher_education_1568037357.pdf

O'Donnell, V. L., & Tobbell, J. (2007). The transition of adult students to higher education: Legitimate peripheral participation in a community of practice? *Adult Education Quarterly, 57*(4), 312–328.

O'Shea, S. (2015). Arriving, surviving, and succeeding: First-in-family women and their experiences of transitioning into the first year of university. *Journal of College Student Development, 56*(5), 499–517.

O'Shea, S. (2016). Avoiding the manufacture of 'sameness': First-in-family students, cultural capital and the higher education environment. *Higher Education, 72*, 59–78.

Ogilvie, A. M., & Knight, D. B. (2021). Post-transfer transition experiences for engineering transfer students. *Journal of College Student Retention: Research, Theory & Practice, 23*(2), 292–321.

Onimus, L. M., & Strawser, J. A. (2021). Elevating assessment processes through stakeholder engagement. In J. M. Souza & T. A. Rose (Eds.), *Exemplars of assessment in higher education: Diverse approaches to addressing accreditation standards*. Stylus.

Orsmond, P., Merry, S., & Callaghan, A. (2013). Communities of practice and ways to learning: Charting the progress of biology undergraduates. *Studies in Higher Education, 38*(6), 890–906.

Oxendine, S. D., Taub, D. J., & Cain, E. J. (2020). Factors related to Native American students' perceptions of campus culture. *Journal of College Student Development, 61*(3), 267–280.

Pace, C. R. (1982). *Achievement and the quality of student effort*. National Commission on Excellence in Education.

Pace, D. (2017, January). *Focus on teaching pre-conference workshop sponsored by the International Society for the Scholarship of Teaching and Learning in History* [Paper presentation]. American Historical Association 2017 Annual Meeting, Denver, CO, United States.

Palbusa, J. A., & Gauvain, M. (2017). Parent–student communication about college and freshman grades in first-generation and non-first-generation students. *Journal of College Student Development, 58*(1), 107–112.

Pallas, A. M. (2003). Educational transitions, trajectories, and pathways. In J. T. Mortimer and M. J. Shanahan (Eds.), *Handbook of the life course* (pp. 165-184). Plenum.

Palmer, M., O'Kane, P., & Owens, M. (2009). Betwixt spaces: Student accounts of turning point experiences in the first-year transition. *Studies in Higher Education, 34*(1), 37–54.

Palmer, P. J. (1993). *To know as we are known: Education as a spiritual journey.* Harper Collins.

Park, J. J., Kim, Y. K., Lue, K., & Parikh, R. M. (2022). What's next? Soon-to-be STEM graduates on their post-graduate plans. *Research in Higher Education*, 1–25.

Parks, S. D. (2000). *Big questions, worthy dreams: Mentoring young adults in their search for meaning, purpose, and faith.* Jossey-Bass.

Parrish, P. E. (2009). Aesthetic principles for instructional design. *Education Tech Research Development, 57,* 511–528.

Pascarella, E. T., & Terenzini, P. T. (2005). *How college affects students: A third decade of research, Volume 2.* Jossey-Bass.

Pérez II, D. (2017). In pursuit of success: Latino male college students exercising academic determination and community cultural wealth. *Journal of College Student Development, 58*(2), 123–140.

Pérez, D., Zamora, B. T., & Pontious, M. W. (2018). Capitalizing on interpersonal thriving: Exploring the community cultural wealth in Latino undergraduate men's peer networks. *Journal of The First-Year Experience & Students in Transition, 30*(1), 11–31.

Perez, M. (2020). An examination of university sophomore students' thriving factors, second-year experiences, and student success outcomes. *Research Issues in Contemporary Education, 5*(1), 1–24.

Perna, L. W. (2006). Studying college access and choice: A proposed conceptual model. In J. Smart (Ed.), *Higher education: Handbook of theory and research* (Vol. 21, pp. 99–1157). Springer.

Pike, G. R., & Robbins, K. R. (2020). Using panel data to identify the effects of institutional characteristics, cohort characteristics, and institutional actions on graduation rates. *Research in Higher Education, 61*(4), 485–509.

Pitstick, V. (2018). The Ohio State University's Second-Year Transformational Experience Program. *New Directions for Higher Education, 183,* 97–107.

Pokorny, H., Holley, D., & Kane, S. (2017). Commuting, transitions and belonging: The experiences of students living at home in their first year at university. *Higher Education, 74*(3), 543–558.

Quaye, S. J., Harper, S. R., & Pendakur, S. L. (Eds.). (2019). *Student engagement in higher education: Theoretical perspectives and practical approaches for diverse populations.* Routledge.

Quinn, J. (2010). Rethinking 'failed transitions' to higher education. In K. Ecclestone, G. Biesta, & M. Hughes (Eds.). *Transitions and learning through the lifecourse* (pp. 118–29). Routledge.

Rask, K. (2010). Attrition in STEM fields at a liberal arts college: The importance of grades and pre-collegiate preferences. *Economics of Education Review, 29*(6), 892–900.

Rendón, L. I. (1994). Validating culturally diverse students: Toward a new model of learning and student development *Innovative Higher Education, 19*(1), 23–32.

Renn, K. A., & Arnold, K. D. (2003). Reconceptualizing research on college student peer culture. *The Journal of Higher Education, 74*(3), 261–291.

Richards, B. N. (2022). Help-seeking behaviors as cultural capital: Cultural guides and the transition from high school to college among low-income first generation students. *Social Problems, 69*(1), 241–260.

Roberts, M. (2023, February 3). *Giving students choices and listening to their voices: Self-directed placement & student success* [Keynote address]. 2023 Annual Conference on the First-Year Experience, Los Angeles, CA, United States.

Rodriguez, A. A., & Mallinckrodt, B. (2021). Native American-identified students' transition to college: A theoretical model of coping challenges and resources. *Journal of College Student Retention: Research, Theory & Practice, 23*(1), 96–117.

Rogerson, C. L., & Poock, M. C. (2013). Differences in populating first year seminars and the impact on retention and course effectiveness. *Journal of College Student Retention: Research, Theory & Practice, 15*(2), 157–172.

Rucks-Ahidiana, Z., & Bork, R. H. (2020). How relationships support and inform the transition to community college. *Research in Higher Education, 61*(5), 588–602.

Rusbult, C. E., & Arriaga, X. B. (1997). Interdependence theory. In S. Duck (Ed.), *Handbook of personal relationships: Theory, research, and interventions* (2nd ed., pp. 221–249). Wiley.

Salancik, G. R., & Pfeffer, J. (1977). Who gets power—and how they hold on to it: A strategic-contingency model of power. *Organizational Dynamics, 5*(3), 3–21.

Salusky, I., Monjaras-Gaytan, L., Ulerio, G., Forbes, N., Perron, G., & Raposa, E. (2022). The formation and role of social belonging in on-campus integration of diverse first-generation college students. *Journal of College Student Retention: Research, Theory & Practice, Advance online publication.* https://doi.org/10.1177/15210251221092709

Sanabria, T., Penner, A., & Domina, T. (2020). Failing at remediation? College remedial coursetaking, failure and long-term student outcomes. *Research in Higher Education, 61*(4), 459–484.

Sanagavarapu, P., Abraham, J., & Taylor, E. (2019). Development and validation of a scale to measure first year students' transitional challenges, wellbeing, help-seeking, and adjustments in an Australian university. *Higher Education, 77*(4), 695–715.

Sanders, M. (2018). *Becoming a learner: Realizing the opportunity of education* (2nd ed.). Hayden-McNeil.

Sanford, N. (1967). *Where colleges fail: A study of the student as a person.* Jossey-Bass.

Sansone, V. A., & Segura, J. S. T. (2020). Exploring factors contributing to college success among student veteran transfers at a four-year university. *The Review of Higher Education, 43*(3), 888–916.

Savage, M. W., Strom, R. E., Ebesu Hubbard, A. S., & Aune, K. S. (2019). Commitment in college student persistence. *Journal of College Student Retention: Research, Theory & Practice, 21*(2), 242–264.

Schaeper, H. (2020). The first year in higher education: The role of individual factors and the learning environment for academic integration. *Higher Education, 79*(1), 95–110.

Schaller, M. A. (2005). Wandering and wondering: Traversing the uneven terrain of the second college year. *About Campus, 10*(3), 17–24.

Schaller, M. A. (2010). Understanding the impact of the second year of college. In M. S. Hunter, B. F. Tobolowsky, J. N. Gardner, S. E. Evenbeck, J. A. Pattengale, M. A. Schaller, & L. A. Schreiner (Eds.), *Helping sophomores succeed: Understanding and improving the second-year experience* (pp. 13–29). Jossey-Bass.

Schaller, M. A. (2018). Intentional design of the college sophomore year. *New Directions for Higher Education, 183*, 23–34.

Schlossberg, N. K. (1981). A model for analyzing human adaptation to transition. *The Counseling Psychologist, 9*(2), 2–18.

Schlossberg, N. K., Lynch, A. Q., and Checkering, A. W. (1989). *Improving higher education environments for adults.* Jossey-Bass.

Schlossberg, N. K., Waters, E., & Goodman, J. (1995). *Counseling adults in transition* (2nd ed.). Springer.

Schooler, S. D. (2014). Native American college student transition theory. *College Student Affairs Leadership, 1*(1), 1–8. https://scholarworks.gvsu.edu/csal/vol1/iss1/1/

Schreiner, L. A. (2010). The "thriving quotient": A new vision for student success. *About Campus, 15*(2), 2–10.

Schreiner, L. A. (2018). Thriving in the second year of college: Pathways to success. *New Directions for Higher Education, 2018*(183), 9–21.

Schreiner, L. A. (2020). From surviving to thriving during transitions. In L. A. Schreiner, M. C. Louis, & D. D. Nelson (Eds.). *Thriving in transitions: A research-based approach to college student success* (2nd ed.). University of South Carolina, National Resource Center for The First-Year Experience and Students in Transition.

Schreiner, L. A., Louis, M. C., & Nelson, D. D. (Eds.). (2020a). *Thriving in transitions: A research-based approach to college student success* (2nd ed.). University of South Carolina, National Resource Center for The First-Year Experience and Students in Transition.

Schreiner, L. A., Pullins, T., & McIntosh, E. J. (2020b). Beyond sophomore survival. In L. A. Schreiner, M. C. Louis, & D. D. Nelson (Eds.), *Thriving in transitions: A research-based approach to college student success* (2nd ed.). University of South Carolina, National Resource Center for The First-Year Experience & Students in Transition.

Scruggs, S., Dong, S., Ducatt, S., Mitchell, J., & Davis, W. (2021). Impact of high school transition and accommodation experience on student involvement in college. *Journal of Postsecondary Education and Disability, 34*(2), 179–190.

Seifert, T. A., Oliveri, C., & Shaw, C. A. (2019). First year research experience (FYRE): Bringing research to new undergraduates. *New Directions for Higher Education, 2019*(188), 71–80.

Selznick, B. S., & Mayhew, M. J. (2019). Developing first-year students' innovation capacities. *The Review of Higher Education, 42*(4), 1607–1634.

Sfard, A. (1998). On two metaphors for learning and the dangers of choosing just one, *Educational Researcher, 27*(2), 4–13

Sharma, G., & Yukhymenko-Lescroart, M. (2018). The relationship between college students' sense of purpose and degree commitment. *Journal of College Student Development, 59*(4), 486–491.

Shim, S. S., Wang, C., Makara, K. A., Xu, X. G., Xie, L. N., & Zhong, M. (2017). College students' social goals and psychological adjustment: Mediation via emotion regulation. *Journal of College Student Development, 58*(8), 1237–1255.

Shim, W. J., & Perez, R. J. (2018). A multi-level examination of first-year students' openness to diversity and challenge. *The Journal of Higher Education, 89*(4), 453–477.

Shirley, M. (2021). Work and race matters: Examining the relationship between two critical factors of college completion at four-year institutions. *The Review of Higher Education, 44*(4), 523–554.

Shook, J. L., & Keup, J. R. (2012). The benefits of peer leader programs: An overview from the literature. *New Directions for Higher Education, 2012*(157), 5–16.

Silver, B. R. (2020). *The cost of inclusion: How student conformity leads to inequality on college campuses.* University of Chicago Press.

Sisk, V. F., Burgoyne, A. P., Sun, J., Butler, J. L., & Macnamara, B. N. (2018). To what extent and under which circumstances are growth mind-sets important to academic achievement? *Two meta-analyses. Psychological Science, 29*(4), 1–23.

Skipper, T. L. (Ed.). (2019). *Aligning institutional support for student success: Case studies of sophomore-year initiatives* (Research Report No. 10). University of South Carolina, National Resource Center for The First-Year Experience & Students in Transition.

Skolnik, M. L. (2010). Quality assurance in higher education as a political process. *Higher Education Management and Policy, 22*(1), 1–20.

Smith, D. I. (2009). Changes in transitions: The role of mobility, class and gender. *Journal of Education and Work, 22*(5), 369–390.

Smith, K. N., & Gayles, J. G. (2017). "Setting up for the next big thing": Undergraduate women engineering students' postbaccalaureate career decisions. *Journal of College Student Development, 58*(8), 1201–1217.

Smith, R. A. (2018). Connective segregation: Residential learning communities as networks of engagement. *The Review of Higher Education, 42*(1), 1–27.

Speckman, M. (2016). First-year village: Experimenting with an African model for first-year adjustment and support in South Africa. *New Directions for Higher Education, 2016*(175), 33–39.

St. Pierre, E. A. (2015). Writing as method. In G. Ritzer (Ed.), *The Blackwell encyclopedia of sociology.* John Wiley & Sons.

St. Pierre, E. A. (2016). The empirical and the new empiricisms. *Cultural Studies <-> Critical Methodologies, 16*(2), 111–124.

Stone, S. L. (2017). Internal voices, external constraints: Exploring the impact of military service on student development. *Journal of College Student Development, 58*(3), 365–384.

Strayhorn, T. L. (2012). Exploring the impact of Facebook and Myspace use on first-year students' sense of belonging and persistence decisions. *Journal of College Student Development, 53*(6), 783–796.

Strayhorn, T. L. (2018). *College students' sense of belonging: A key to educational success for all students* (2nd ed.). Routledge.

Suchan, J. J. (2016). *Exploring the experience of academic suspension and subsequent academic resilience for college students who were reinstated to the institution: A phenomenological analysis* [Doctoral dissertation, Iowa State University]. Iowa State University Digital Repository. https://lib.dr.iastate.edu/etd/15816

Swing, R. L., & Ross, L. E. (2016). A new vision for institutional research. *Change: The Magazine of Higher Learning, 48*(2), 6–13.

Tachine, A. R., Cabrera, N. L., & Yellow Bird, E. (2017). Home away from home: Native American students' sense of belonging during their first year in college. *The Journal of Higher Education, 88*(5), 785–807.

Taylor, A., Parks, R., & Edwards, A. (2016). Challenges on the front lines: Serving today's student veterans. *College and University, 91*(4), 47–60.

Taylor, C. A., & Harris-Evans, J. (2018). Reconceptualising transition to higher education with Deleuze and Guattari. *Studies in Higher Education, 43*(7), 1254–1267.

Tazewell, S. (2022). Using a funds of knowledge approach to engage diverse cohorts through active and personally relevant learning. In G. Crimmins (Ed.), *Strategies for supporting inclusion and diversity in the academy: Higher education, aspiration and inequality* (2nd ed.). Palgrave Macmillan.

Terenzini, P. T., Rendon, L. I., Lee Upcraft, M., Millar, S. B., Allison, K. W., Gregg, P. L., & Jalomo, R. (1994). The transition to college: Diverse students, diverse stories. *Research in Higher Education, 35*, 57–73.

Thaler, R. H., & Sunstein, C. R. (2008). *Nudge: Improving decisions about health, wealth, and happiness.* Penguin.

Tholen, R., Wouters, E., Ponnet, K., de Bruyn, S., & Van Hal, G. (2022). Academic stress, anxiety, and depression among Flemish first-year students: The mediating role of sense of belonging. *Journal of College Student Development, 63*(2), 200–217.

Tierney, W. G. (1992). An anthropological analysis of student participation in college. *The Journal of Higher Education, 63*(6), 603–618.

Tierney, W. G., & Venegas, K. M. (2009). Finding money on the table: Information, financial aid, and access to college. *The Journal of Higher Education, 80*(4), 363–388.

Tinto, V. (1975). Dropout from higher education: A theoretical synthesis of recent research. *Review of Educational Research, 45*(1), 89–125.

Tinto, V. (1993). *Leaving college: Rethinking the causes and cures of student attrition* (2nd ed.). University of Chicago.

Tinto, V. (2012). *Completing college: Rethinking institutional action.* University of Chicago Press.

Tobbell, J., & O'Donnell, V. (2005, September 8-9). *Theorising educational transitions: Communities, practice and participation* [Paper presentation]. Conference on Sociocultural Theory in Educational Research and Practice, University of Manchester, Manchester, UK. http://eprints.hud.ac.uk/id/eprint/7743/

Tovar, E., & Simon, M. A. (2006). Academic probation as a dangerous opportunity: Factors influencing diverse college students' success. *Community College Journal of Research and Practice, 30*(7), 547–564.

Trolian, T. L. (2019). Predicting student involvement in the first year of college: The influence of students' precollege professional and career attitudes. *Journal of College Student Development, 60*(1), 120–127.

Turk, J. M., & González Canché, M. S. (2019). On-campus housing's impact on degree completion and upward transfer in the community college sector: A comprehensive quasi-experimental analysis. *The Journal of Higher Education, 90*(2), 244–271.

Turner, L., & Tobbell, J. (2018). Learner identity and transition: An ethnographic exploration of undergraduate trajectories. *Journal of Further and Higher Education, 42*(5), 708–720.

U.S. Department of Education. (2003). *Dual enrollment: Accelerating the transition to college* [High School Leadership Summit Issue Paper]. Author. https://brightspotcdn.byu.edu/88/b8/f457e4444cba940a88adac44b877/doe-duel-enrollement.pdf

Upcraft, M. L., Gardner, J. N., & Barefoot, B. O. (2005). *Challenging and supporting the first-year student: A handbook for improving the first year of college.* Jossey-Bass.

Vaccaro, A., Kimball, E., Newman, B. M., Moore, A., & Troiano, P. F. (2019). Collegiate purpose development at the intersections of disability and social class habitus. *The Review of Higher Education, 43*(1), 403–426.

Vacchi, D. T., & Berger, J. B. (2014). Student veterans in higher education. In M. B. Paulsen (Ed.), *Higher education: Handbook of theory and research* (Vol. 29, pp. 93–151). Springer, Dordrecht.

Vetter, M., Schreiner, L., & Jaworski, B. (2019). Faculty attitudes and behaviors that contribute to thriving in first-year students of color. *Journal of the First-Year Experience & Students in Transition, 31*(1), 9–28.

Vogelgesang, L. J., & Astin, A. W. (2000). Comparing the effects of community service and service-learning. *Michigan Journal of Community Service Learning, 7*(1).

Vygotsky, L. S. (1978). *Mind in society: The development of higher psychological processes.* Harvard University Press.

Wall, A. F., Hursh, D., & Rodgers III, J. W. (2014). Assessment for whom: Repositioning higher education assessment as an ethical and value-focused social practice. *Research & Practice in Assessment, 9*, 5–17.

Waltenbury, M., Brady, S., Gallo, M., Redmond, N., Draper, S., & Fricker, T. (2018). *Academic probation: Evaluating the impact of academic standing notification letters on students.* Higher Education Quality Council of Ontario.

Walton, G. M., & Cohen, G. L. (2007). A question of belonging: Race, social fit, and achievement. *Journal of Personality and Social Psychology, 92*(1), 82–96.

Wang, X. (2017). Toward a holistic theoretical model of momentum for community college student success. In M. B. Paulsen (Ed.), *Higher education: Handbook of theory and research,* (Vol. 32, pp. 259–308).

Wang, X., Lee, Y., & Wickersham, K. (2019). Exploring the relationship between longitudinal course-taking patterns and in-state transfer into STEM fields of study. *The Journal of Higher Education, 90*(2), 272–297.

Weidman, J. (1989). Undergraduate socialization: A conceptual approach. In J. C. Weidman (Ed.), *Higher education: Handbook of theory and research, 5*(2), 289–322.

Wellman, J. V. (2010). *Connecting the dots between learning and resources.* NILOA Occasional Paper, 3.

Wenger, E. (1998). *Communities of practice: Learning, meaning, and identity.* Cambridge University.

Weston, T. J., Seymour, E., Koch, A. K., & Drake, B. M. (2019). Weed-out classes and their consequences. In E. Seymour and A. B. Hunter (Eds.), *Talking about leaving revisited: Persistence, relocation, and loss in undergraduate STEM education* (pp. 197–243). Springer.

Weuffen, S., Fotinatos, N., & Andrews, T. (2021). Evaluating sociocultural influences affecting participation and understanding of academic support services and programs (SSPs): Impacts on notions of attrition, retention, and success in higher education. *Journal of College Student Retention: Research, Theory & Practice, 23*(1), 118–138.

Wiley (2023). *The state of the student: Adjusting to the "new normal" … and all that comes with it.* https://www.wiley.com/en-us/network/trending-stories/the-state-of-the-student-adjusting-to-the-new-normal-and-all-that-comes-with-it

Wilson, S. P., Gore, J. S., Renfro, A., Blake, M., Muncie, E., & Treadway, J. (2018). The tether to home, university connectedness, and the Appalachian student. *Journal of College Student Retention: Research, Theory & Practice, 20*(1), 139–160.

Wolniak, G. C. (2016). Examining STEM bachelor's degree completion for students with differing propensities at college entry. *Journal of College Student Retention: Research, Theory & Practice, 18*(3), 287–309.

Worth, N. (2009). Understanding youth transition as 'becoming': Identity, time and futurity. *Geoforum, 40*(6), 1050–1060.

Xu, D., Jaggars, S. S., Fletcher, J., & Fink, J. E. (2018). Are community college transfer students "a good bet" for 4-year admissions? Comparing academic and labor-market outcomes between transfer and native 4-year college students. *The Journal of Higher Education, 89*(4), 478–502.

Xu, D., Solanki, S., & Harlow, A. (2020). Examining the relationship between 2-year college entry and baccalaureate aspirants' academic and labor market outcomes: Impacts, heterogeneity, and mechanisms. *Research in Higher Education, 61*, 297–329.

Yanchar, S. C., & Gabbitas, B. W. (2011). Between eclecticism and orthodoxy in instructional design. *Educational Technology Research and Development, 59*, 383–398.

Yanchar, S. C., Spackman, J. S., & Faulconer, J. E. (2013). Learning as embodied familiarization. *Journal of Theoretical and Philosophical Psychology, 33*(4), 216–232.

Yao, C. W. (2015). Sense of belonging in international students: Making the case against integration to US institutions of higher education. *Journal of Comparative & International Higher Education, 7*(Spring), 6–10.

Yeager, D. S., Walton, G. M., Brady, S. T., Akcinar, E. N., Paunesku, D., Keane, L., Kamentz, D., Ritter, G., Duckworth, A. L., Urstein, R., Gomez, E. M., Markus, H. R., Cohen, G. L., & Dweck, C. S. (2016). *Teaching a lay theory before college narrows achievement gaps at scale.* Proceedings of the National Academy of Sciences, USA, 113(24), E3341-E3348. https://doi.org/10.1073/pnas.1524360113

Yosso, T. J. (2005). Whose culture has capital? A critical race theory discussion of community cultural wealth. *Race ethnicity and education, 8*(1), 69–91.

Young, D. G. (2016). The case for an integrated approach to transition programmes at South Africa's higher education institutions. *Journal of Student Affairs in Africa, 4*(1), 17–32.

Young, D. G. (2018). Outcomes assessment and sophomore programs: How assessment as organizational learning can improve institutional integrity. *New Directions for Higher Education, 2018*(183), 47–57.

Young, D. G. (Ed.). (2019). *2017 National Survey on The First-Year Experience: Structures for supporting student success* (Research Reports on College Transitions No. 9). University of South Carolina, National Resource Center for The First-Year Experience & Students in Transition.

Young, D. G. (2020). Is first-year seminar type predictive of institutional retention rates? *Journal of College Student Development, 61*(3), 379–390.

Young, D. G., Chung, J. K., Hoffman, D. E., & Bronkema, R. (2017). *2016 National Survey of Senior Capstone Experiences: Expanding our understanding of culminating experiences* (Research Reports on College Transitions No. 8). University of South Carolina, National Resource Center for The First-Year Experience & Students in Transition.

Young, D. G., Schreiner, L. A., & McIntosh, E. J. (2015). *Investigating sophomore student success: The National Survey of Sophomore-Year Initiatives and the Sophomore Experiences Survey – 2014* (Research Report No. 6). National Resource Center for The First-Year Experience and Students in Transition, University of South Carolina.

Young, D. G., & Weigel, D. (2022). Assessing student probation and academic recovery initiatives. In M. T. Dial (Ed.), *Academic recovery: Supporting students on academic probation*. University of South Carolina, National Resource Center for the First-Year Experience & Students in Transition.

Zerquera, D. D. (2019). The problem with the prestige pursuit: The effects of striving on access for Black and Latino students at urban-serving research universities. *The Review of Higher Education, 42*(5), 393–424.

Zerquera, D. D., Ziskin, M., & Torres, V. (2018). Faculty views of "nontraditional" students: Aligning perspectives for student success. *Journal of College Student Retention: Research, Theory & Practice, 20*(1), 29–46.

Zhang, Y. L., Adamuti-Trache, M., & Connolly, J. (2019). From community college attendants to baccalaureate recipients: A planned behavior model for transfer students in STEM fields of study. *The Journal of Higher Education, 90*(3), 373–401.

ABOUT THE AUTHORS

Dallin George Young

Dr. Dallin George Young is an assistant professor in College Student Affairs Administration (CSAA) and Student Affairs Leadership (SAL) at the University of Georgia. His research agenda includes using activity-based theoretical perspectives to interrogate student transitions into the academy; how graduate and professional students learn the rules, knowledge, and culture of their aspirational professional communities; and the impacts of educational structures on the success of these transitions, including investigating differential effects on student populations.

Bryce D. Bunting

Dr. Bryce D. Bunting is an associate clinical professor in Student Development Services, the Assistant Dean of Undergraduate Education, and Director of the First-Year Experience at Brigham Young University (BYU). His research agenda is focused on using instructional design to inform the development of high-impact and transformative learning experiences in the first year of college; the impact of peer leadership on those who serve as peer leaders; and the application of learning theory to rethinking and redesigning college transition programming.

INDEX

ACPA Directorate Board for the
Commission on Admissions, Orientation,
and First-Year Experience, 51
adaptive challenges, transitions and, 77
adjustment
    challenges with transitions as, 18–19
    shifting to transitions as becoming
    from, 117
    as transition lens, relationships and,
    102–3
    transitions as, 17–18, 21*t*, 24–5*t*,
    29–31*t*
administrators. *See also* institutional leaders;
staff
    student being and becoming and, 90
adult learners, 20, 21–3, 28
advisers. *See* academic advisors
African American students, 94–8. *See also*
Black students; students of color
agency. *See also* co-agency (co-agentic
spaces)
    academic probation and, 129
    CCBC students and, 95
    dialectic of institutional and student,
    38–40
    equity-minded practices and, 97
    movement or adjustment and stability
    and, 21*t*
    pathways and, 24
    student, transition programs and, 88
    student, views of critical junctures and,
    20
    terminology choices and, 55
    transitions as becoming and, 35*t*
    transitions as development and, 25*t*
    transitions as sociocultural process and,
    30*t*
    understanding co-agentic definitions of
    success and, 140

Annual Conference on The First-Year
Experience, 62
anxiety, transitions as becoming and, 32
Anzaldúa, G., 48
assessment
    community, participation, and
    becoming in transitions and, 85
    considerations, 92–4
    contextualized learning and, 118
    design factors, 91
    under developmental perspective, 137
    example, 91–2
    experimenting with, 99
    key questions for, 94
assessment panels, at Seton Hall University,
91–2
Association for the Study of Higher
Education, xv
Attinasi, L. C., 2–3, 33
authenticity (authentic practices), 70, 90,
98, 110

B

Baker, S., 33
Barefoot, B., 3
barely surviving, after first-year experience,
5
Barnett, R., 77
Bassett, B. S., 27
Baxter Magolda, M. B., 77, 86
Bean, J. P., 26
becoming. *See also* transitions as becoming
    academic writing in undergraduate
    research and, 88–9
    across place and time, 74–5
    assessment and, 93
    communities of practice and, 98, 101
    components to understanding
    supporting, as process of, 10